William Gray Murray rose to positions of great importance despite his humble beginnings. Prior to the Civil War, he led a distinguished life, as both a soldier—serving with distinction in the Mexican War—and as postmaster of Blair County, Pennsylvania. As colonel of the 84th Pennsylvania Volunteer Infantry, Murray ably led his regiment at Hancock and played a leading role in foiling the plans of Stonewall Jackson. Murray fell at the head of his regiment at the Battle of Kernstown.

Ultimate Sacrifice at the Battle of Kernstown relies heavily on unpublished and obscure sources, including newspaper articles and soldiers' diaries and pension files. The book offers a fascinating glimpse not only of a largely forgotten life but also into the internal politics and feuds of an early war Pennsylvania regiment.

Ultimate Sacrifice at the Battle of Kernstown

William Gray Murray, First Pennsylvania Colonel to Die in the American Civil War

By
Roderick Rodgers Gainer Jr.

White Mane Books
Shippensburg, Pennsylvania

Copyright © 2007 by Roderick Rodgers Gainer, Jr.

ALL RIGHTS RESERVED—No part of this book may be reproduced in any form without permission in writing from the publisher, except by a reviewer who wishes to quote brief passages in connection with a review.

The acid-free paper used in this book meets the guidelines for permanence and durability of the Committee on Production Guidelines for Book Longevity of the Council on Library Resources.

For a complete list of available publications
please write
White Mane Books
Division of White Mane Publishing Company, Inc.
P.O. Box 708
Shippensburg, PA 17257-0708 USA

Library of Congress Cataloging-in-Publication Data

Gainer, Roderick Rodgers, 1965-
  Ultimate sacrifice at the Battle of Kernstown : William Gray Murray, first Pennsylvania colonel to die in the American Civil War / by Roderick Rodgers Gainer Jr.
    p. cm.
  Includes bibliographical references and index.
  ISBN-13: 978-1-57249-391-9 (pbk. : alk. paper)
  ISBN-10: 1-57249-391-7 (pbk. : alk. paper)
  1. Murray, William Gray, 1825-1862. 2. Murray, William Gray, 1825-1862--Death and burial. 3. United States. Army. Pennsylvania Infantry Regiment, 84th (1861-1865) 4. Kernstown, 1st Battle of, Winchester, Va., 1862. 5. United States. Army—Officers—Biography. 6. Soldiers—Pennsylvania—Biography. 7. Pennsylvania—History—Civil War, 1861-1865--Regimental histories. 8. United States—History—Civil War, 1861-1865--Regimental histories. I. Title.
  E527.584th .G35 2007
  973.7'31092--dc22
  [B]

2006033491

PRINTED IN THE UNITED STATES OF AMERICA

*To my wife Linda,
my daughter Elizabeth, and
to Captain Patrick Gallagher
of the 84th, who like his friend
Murray, fell at Kernstown.*

CONTENTS

Preface		vii
Acknowledgments		ix
Chapter 1	Early Life	1
Chapter 2	Murray Enlists	3
Chapter 3	To the Halls of the Montezumas	11
Chapter 4	A Civilian Again	21
Chapter 5	The 84th Is Formed	27
Chapter 6	Hancock	33
Chapter 7	Winter Activities	45
Chapter 8	Trouble at Winchester	49
Chapter 9	Kernstown	53
Chapter 10	Murray's Return	63
Epilogue		67
Appendixes		69
Notes		73
Bibliography		79
Index		83

PREFACE

Like all great conflicts, the Civil War produced many heroes. Some of these heroes are immortalized in bronze, keeping watch over quiet battlefields or town squares. Others are remembered in biographies and histories. Sadly, a great number of distinguished men and women of the period are all but forgotten today. For example, the Baker Mansion, in Altoona, Pennsylvania, houses a nice selection of memorabilia celebrating that Blair County's history. Among the items in the collection are a horse's skull, and a few images of just such a forgotten hero. These items and a battered tombstone in a dilapidated cemetery are all that remain of William Gray Murray.

Murray was a distinguished citizen, a Mexican War hero, and the postmaster of Blair County from 1852 to 1860. When the Civil War broke out, he volunteered his services and became the colonel of the 84th Pennsylvania Volunteer Infantry. Less than six months later, at the Battle of Kernstown, William Gray Murray became the first Pennsylvania colonel to die in battle. Other soldiers had more distinguished careers than Murray, and many served as bravely. Nonetheless, Murray's story deserves to be better known. He proved a courageous officer, and his death a major event in early war Pennsylvania. In many ways, Murray's death signified the great demographic destruction that befell not only Pennsylvania but all the participating states of the American Civil War.

Acknowledgments

I owe many people a debt of gratitude for this little work. Timothy C. Van Scoyoc of the Blair County Historical Society proved invaluable in tracking down information, as well as providing many of the images in this book. Gary Ecelbarger and Scott Patchan, two great friends and fellow travelers on the "cannonball circuit," provided both suggestions and companionship on numerous research trips, staff rides, and tours over the years. Dave Richards, *the* leading expert on the 84th Pennsylvania Volunteer Infantry, also offered numerous insights, as well as his encyclopedic knowledge of the regiment during the preparation of this work. My many mentors, especially in graduate school, also merit special mention. Dr. Joseph Harsh will always be a major influence in my life. He taught me the meaning of scholarship. Tom Clemens likewise has proved a valuable friend, and his great knowledge of the war leaves me both humbled and a tad jealous. Sam Doss, another good friend, also deserves special mention. My family has always been a source of endless inspiration. Mom, Joe, Dad, Debbie, Ashley, Jeff, and Amanda, thank you all. Lastly, special thanks to my beautiful wife, who so patiently allows my many trips and projects. She has truly blessed my life.

CHAPTER 1
Early Life

William Gray Murray was born on July 25, 1825, in the town of Longford in Central Ireland. His parents were John and Sarah (Gray) Murray.[1] Soon after giving birth to William, Sarah Murray became pregnant again, and nine months later gave birth to a baby girl.

When William Murray turned all of nine months, his father, like many of his countrymen, decided to leave his troubled homeland and seek his fortune in the New World. John Murray bundled up his small family and set sail for America. The Murrays soon arrived in New York. Unlike many of his fellow Irish immigrants, John Murray possessed some education and wealth. He quickly established himself in New York as a "business man."[2]

John Murray soon moved his family a second time. This time the small family settled in Utica, New York. The older Murray, known for his gregarious and open nature, had by this time achieved success. He founded two "mercantile houses," one at Rome, and the other at Canandaigua. John Murray had great skill in business and established himself in his newly adopted country. Soon, his two young sons entered school, and his future seemed secure.[3]

Unfortunately, the Murrays had only a short time to enjoy their happiness. The "Panic of 1837" destroyed their prosperity.

The price of cotton, vital to the United States' mercantile business in the nineteenth century, dropped to half its peak value in 1837. Overspeculation, the cause of so many economic troubles throughout American history, instigated the panic. As the price of cotton plummeted, the American textile business collapsed. Like many others, the Murrays faced ruin and poverty.

Yet, the family persevered, and they again struck out to regain their lost prosperity. John Murray proved nothing if not resourceful and decided that a change of venue would be in his family's best interest. The Murrays moved to Pennsylvania, where they settled first in Lancaster. John soon established himself in the local mercantile business and after a relatively short time regained his fortunes. Despite this success, the old wanderlust soon struck the family, and they again moved, this time to Harrisburg.[4]

During this time, young William fast became a man. He attended school regularly, and underwent training to follow in his father's footsteps as a mercantile businessman. Upon the completion of his schooling, William Murray worked at his father's store in Harrisburg. Soon after, young William transferred to a large mercantile house in New York City in order to better facilitate his apprenticeship in the family business. While William resided in New York, disaster struck his family: John Murray died in the fall of 1844. The loss devastated William and the rest of the family. John Murray had done much to keep his family secure: no easy matter in chaotic mid-nineteenth-century America.[5]

William Murray remained in New York until the spring of 1845, when he took over his father's estate and sought to start his own mercantile business. For the first time in his life, William Gray Murray worked for himself. By all appearances, it appeared that Murray would enjoy a long and successful life, yet clouds began to appear on the American horizon.

Chapter 2
Murray Enlists

The United States, proudly proclaiming her "manifest destiny," sought to expand. Newspapers all over the U.S. called for a push to the West. Like the United States, Mexico also wished to expand and solidify her borders. The stage had been set for the inevitable conflict between the two young nations.

The admission of Texas into the Union in 1845 did not sit well with Mexico. The successful Texas Revolution in 1836 had cost Mexico in both land and pride. For nearly ten years, the future of the "Lone Star Republic" hung in the balance as slave holders in the U.S. worked to annex Texas, thus creating another slave state. Naturally, the Mexican government wished to reclaim her former rebellious state. When the United States annexed Texas into the Union at the behest of President John Tyler in 1845, it proved more than the proud government of Mexico could stand.

The storm broke at Matamoras on April 25, 1846. Mexican army units attacked U.S. Regulars along the Texas border. Less than one month later, the United States declared war.

The United States met with nothing but success in the first part of the war. Zachary Taylor won two smashing victories, Palo Alto and Resaca de la Palma, in northern Mexico. Temporary hopes for peace were dashed, however, when Mexico elected

Antonio Lopez de Santa Anna as president and launched a campaign against Taylor. Taylor succeeded in defeating Santa Anna at Buena Vista. At the same time, California, with the help of many U.S. citizens and soldiers, also broke away from Mexico and sought to join the United States. The war then ground down to a temporary standstill as Taylor, against President James Polk's wishes, signed an armistice. Eventually the U.S. government, wanting far more than just Texas, cancelled the peace agreement. Both sides gathered their strength for a renewal of the war.

Back in Harrisburg, twenty-two-year-old William Murray followed the course of the war with great interest. When news came of a renewal of hostilities, Murray put aside his business practice and decided to join his state's forces. On December 6, 1846, William Gray Murray enlisted into the army of the United States.[1]

Murray mustered into a company known as the "Cameron Guards." He enlisted for the "duration of the war." Captain Edward C. Williams raised the Cameron Guards, named for Senator Simon Cameron. The company had a strength of around ninety-five men. Murray's company marched to Pittsburgh, where it reorganized as Company G of the 2nd Pennsylvania Volunteer Infantry on January 2, 1847.[2]

William Murray, already a successful businessman, excelled as a natural leader. Murray mustered in as a sergeant, even though he had no prior military experience. The young volunteer was certainly physically ready to be a soldier. Years of working in textile mills had toughened Murray's frame, which stood just less than six feet tall. His hazel eyes and brown hair gave him a dashing appearance. Murray's natural gifts would soon be tested. The army slated his regiment to join Winfield Scott's invasion army on its voyage to Mexico.

The 2nd Pennsylvania proved a fine regiment, blessed with several outstanding officers. Colonel William Geary, a very gallant officer, would distinguish himself in the upcoming campaign and in the Civil War. At least eight of its members — like Murray — would fight in the Civil War as Union colonels. Although new to war, Murray enjoyed very good military company.[3]

During Company K's stay in Pittsburgh, a soldier accidentally shot and killed a civilian. Shortly afterwards — no doubt to better regulate the unruly young recruits — the regiment elected its field officers. By the beginning of 1847, the 2nd Pennsylvania Volunteer Infantry prepared to move to the front.[4]

Murray's company set sail on January 8, 1847, aboard the steamer *Anthony Wayne*. Murray now received his introduction to the monotony of military life. The 2nd received strict orders while on board, detailing the new regiment's activities while on the *Anthony Wayne*:

> The Arms will remain boxed, with the exception of those required for guard duty. Squad drills, without arms, will be had daily, at the discretion of the senior officer of the detachment.
>
> Bars, for the sale or distribution of liquor are strictly prohibited by the commanding officer of the Regiment: and officers commanding detachments will be held responsible for any infringement of this order.
>
> No Soldier will be permitted to leave the boat after leaving Pittsburgh, until he arrives at New Orleans.
>
> The senior officer of each detachment will report his arrival at New Orleans to the Quarter Master.
>
> There shall be, daily, five roll-calls: — the first immediately after Reveille; — the second immediately before breakfast; — the third immediately before dinner; — the fourth immediately before retreat; — the fifth immediately after Tattoo.
>
> The senior officer will detail, daily, a police party, whose duty it shall be to superintend the cleanliness of the transport.

> No Revolving Pistols, Bowie Knives, or other Arms, will be allowed to remain in the possession of the soldiers on board the transports...
>
> The commanding officer expects the officers commanding detachments to secure and preserve strict discipline and decorum among the men....[5]

Although subjected to rigorous discipline on the trip, Murray undoubtedly enjoyed the leisurely trip down the great American interior waterways. For the first time in his life, Murray saw the vast American landscape. Between January 14 and 18, the steamers transporting the 2nd Pennsylvania pulled into New Orleans.[6]

The 2nd encamped near the site of the old Battle of New Orleans. Many of the Pennsylvanians were impressed with the battlefield and the nearby city, with its many allures. Others quickly grew bored with camp life.

The soldiers' morale grew with the news that the regiment would soon leave for Mexico. Three transport vessels arrived on January 23 to carry the 2nd to the island of Lobos, a gathering place for General Winfield Scott's growing army. The army assigned Murray's company to the USS *General Veazie*, and the troops boarded on January 24. Stormy weather, however, delayed the passage to Lobos. Unrest festered in the ranks of the Pennsylvanians; deplorable conditions aboard the ships and foul food sapped the troops' spirits. Several soldiers deserted by jumping overboard and swam for "safety" in the harbor. The regiment's officers promised that conditions would improve, but morale remained low.[7]

After about a week, the *General Veazie* and the other transports sailed for the Mississippi Delta. As soon as they arrived, on February 2, bad weather again arose. Severe storms pounded the 2nd Pennsylvania's little transport fleet. One soldier in Company E recalled:

Murray Enlists

The excessive tossing of the vessel affected most of the men with seasickness, and it was one continual sound of puking, spitting, groaning, and laughing mixed with the tumult of the gale.... The gale blew all day and at night was still high. The puking continued with little abatement.[8]

How Murray reacted to all of this is unknown. Used to hard physical labor, and having worked for a number of years in textile mills, this still must have been very different and frustrating for the young sergeant. Undoubtedly, Murray longed to see the shores of Mexico, and dry land.

By February 3, the weather had improved dramatically. The sea calmed, and the sky cleared. Still, many men were caught in a dilemma as they were "unable to remain below on account of stench and very uncomfortable on deck in consequence of the extreme heat" in the words of one soldier.[9]

The Pennsylvanians did not have long to enjoy this brief respite before another gale hit on the tenth. This storm lasted nearly fifty-six hours. Even though the ships soon arrived at their first destination, Tampico, landing proved impossible in such a sea. The fleet sailed on for Lobos.[10]

The 2nd Pennsylvania's transports straggled into Lobos on February 13. Many of the delighted Keystoners began to disembark from their various vessels as soon as they arrived. Murray, within sight of land, must have felt his spirit soar at the thought of planting his feet on terra firma.

Unfortunately, disaster again struck Murray's luckless vessel. One of the soldiers on the *General Veazie* came down with smallpox just as the cursed fleet brought the 2nd Pennsylvania into Lobos. All aboard the *General Veazie* soon found themselves in quarantine.[11]

From the ship, Murray and his companions could look longingly on Lobos, an island rich in vegetation; including a great number of orange and lemon trees. The men saw a great abundance of fish and wildlife as well. The sickening conditions aboard the *General Veazie* stood in stark contrast to the beautiful and exotic tropical island.[12]

While on the *General Veazie*, Murray learned the true life of a soldier. For the first time, Murray witnessed the diametric poles of army life. Camaraderie and discipline, which must have appealed to the businessman in Murray, were countered by the petty tyranny and stupidity of life in the nineteenth-century American army. Geary and a few officers disembarked, but the rest of the regiment remained cooped up in the ship. This must have had a profound effect on Murray. High-ranking officers, not the rank and file, seemed to possess all the privileges. The privates and NCOs suffered most in the day-to-day routine of army life. Murray never forgot this lesson, and it would influence the rest of his military life. By starting out as a noncommissioned officer, Murray would forever hold the welfare of the common soldier in high regard.

As Murray and his shipmates sweltered in the hot Mexican sun aboard their ship, the rest of Scott's army arrived. Regular Army regiments complemented volunteer troops from all over the United States. Regiments from North and South Carolina, New York, Louisiana, and Mississippi arrived on the island for drilling. Although many of these troops later left, the majority of Winfield Scott's army sharpened and honed their military skills at Lobos.

By the end of February, Scott himself arrived. The actual invasion date, aimed at the fortress of Vera Cruz, approached. In late February and early March, Scott's army began to depart for the Mexican mainland. As the last of the army sailed out of sight, the wretched men aboard the *General Veazie* finally landed on the nearly deserted island. Sixteen more men became sick with the dreaded smallpox, and many others fell ill after having been cooped up in the ship. Murray escaped the rigors of his ordeal unscathed, and reported "present for duty" once the three companies formed and took roll on the beach at Lobos.

While Murray waited at Lobos, he applied for an officer's commission in the United States Regulars. By an act of Congress, the recruiting of several new regiments of Regulars commenced. Many of these new outfits consisted of volunteer companies, which soon organized into regular battalions. Unfortunately, too few officers existed to command the new regiments. This created a desperate need for qualified men, and quickly. Murray, his stamina already proven aboard the *General Veazie*, qualified to be an officer in the new U.S. regiments. His business skills, which helped with organization, also helped him to ingratiate himself with the army's command. Murray promptly applied for a commission. On March 5, 1847, Murray heard that his appointment as second lieutenant of the United States Regular Army had been accepted.[13]

A few weeks later, the marooned Pennsylvanians finally received some good news. Vera Cruz had fallen, and the army doctors decided that the smallpox outbreak no longer posed a threat. The Pennsylvanians at Lobos joined the rest of their regiment and Scott's army on April 8, 1847. By this time, Scott had begun advancing overland, leaving Vera Cruz behind. The next day, April 9, Murray received his assignment to Company E of the 11th U.S. Infantry. After waiting so long, Murray set out to witness the war up close, now as a regular.[14]

Chapter 3
To the Halls of the Montezumas

Winfield Scott's campaign to capture Mexico City remains one of the greatest military achievements of the nineteenth century, and arguably the most brilliant campaign in American history. The Americans, operating with a very tenuous supply line and heavily outnumbered, faced a daunting challenge. They faced a tough and experienced foe, on his home soil. Nonetheless, Scott succeeded, and William Gray Murray played a part in it.[1]

Scott's army, roughly ten thousand men, continued its advance into the Mexican interior. On April 16, after bidding his friends in the 2nd Pennsylvania goodbye, Murray left to accept his commission into the Regular Army. The 11th U.S. now occupied the banks along the Rio Grande, prepared to support either Taylor or Scott. In mid-May, the 11th, part of Brigadier General George Cadwalader's brigade, prepared to move to Vera Cruz in order to link up with Scott. Murray prepared to depart for that city to join his new regiment.

The next day, while advancing, Scott's army ran into Santa Anna's entrenchments at Cerro Gordo. After a bloody battle, the Americans succeeded in driving off the Mexicans.[2] Although Murray had "officially" departed his regiment, he may have remained behind to witness the battle. At any rate, Murray soon set off on the fifty-mile journey to Vera Cruz.[3]

Chapter 3

On June 1, Cadwalader's brigade, consisting of the 11th and 14th U.S. Regulars, the U.S. "Voltigeurs" (light troops), and a battery of artillery arrived at Vera Cruz.[4] Again, fortune favored Murray, placing him in a well-officered outfit. Like the 2nd Pennsylvania, many of the 11th U.S.'s officers became important officers in the Civil War. The army soon attached Cadwalader's brigade to Major General Gideon Pillow's division.[5]

Scott's advance, meanwhile, had ground to a halt. Many of Scott's volunteers' twelve-month terms would soon expire. Before Scott could continue his advance, he would have to be heavily reinforced. Thus, Scott had to wait at Puebla until Pillow's division and another could march up from Vera Cruz.

Cadwalader's men advanced from Vera Cruz on June 4 to defend a column of supply wagons destined for Scott's army. During the march, the column battled Mexican guerillas, giving Murray and his comrades their first real taste of combat.

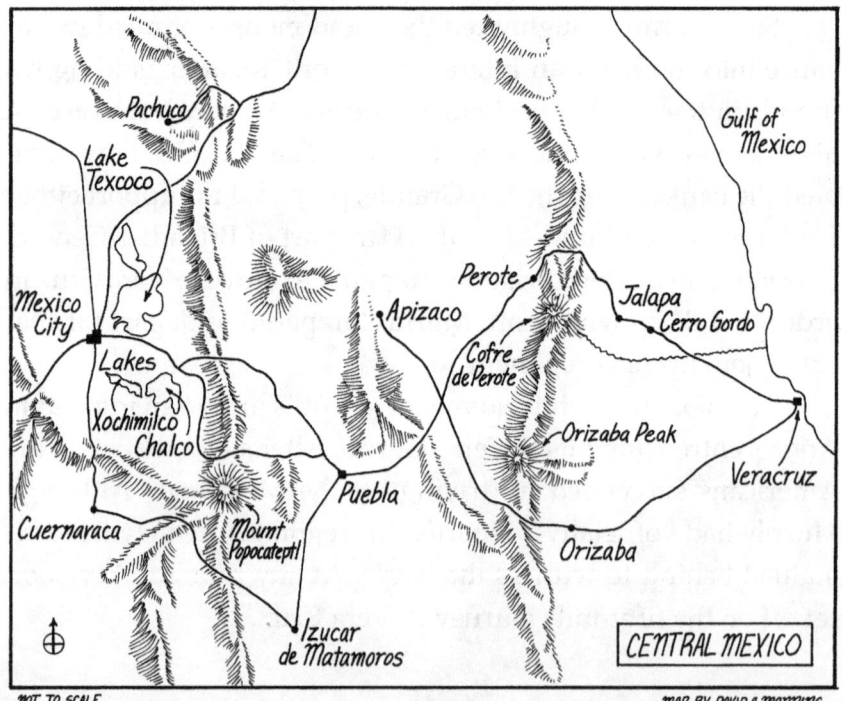

Cadwalader halted his brigade at Perote to await the rest of Pillow's division, which had departed from Vera Cruz on June 8.

Eventually, Pillow's division linked up with the rest of Scott's army at Puebla on August 8, after a very leisurely march. The march into the Valley of Mexico must have been a very interesting experience for young Lieutenant Murray. Guerilla activity somewhat dampened the green 11th's enthusiasm for war, but like most of the young officers on the march, Murray undoubtedly determined to adhere to Scott's adage to "conquer a peace."

Scott's army marched through the Mexican countryside and approached the capital city from the south. As the American army neared the town of San Agustin, fifteen miles south of Mexico City, Cadwalader's brigade skirmished with elements of the Mexican army on August 12. The 11th U.S. participated in this little fight.

Murray had now been in the service of the U.S. Army for nearly nine months. Although he had not seen a great deal of action, the rigors of the campaign had broken many other men down. Lieutenant Murray managed to remain with his unit, proving that he had at least the willpower and physical stamina to be a successful officer.[6]

From San Agustin, Scott advanced his army to the west in an attempt to skirt the Pedregal, an impassable mass of dried lava south of Mexico City. By the evening of August 19, the Americans maneuvered into position. In a daring attack—reconnoitered in part by Robert E. Lee—Pillow's and General David Twiggs' divisions utterly routed a large element of the Mexican army at Contreras. By midday on the twentieth, the Mexican army scampered in full retreat.

Cadwalader's brigade played a very important role in this great victory. Murray, for the first time in the war, participated in a large battle. The Pedregal, the last natural barrier in front of Mexico City, had been bypassed.

Santa Anna's army made another stand at Churubusco, on August 20. The Americans, flushed with victory, pursued the fleeing Mexicans as fast as they could. This time, however, the Mexicans prepared well for the American advance. All through the day, the American army launched repeated assaults down the National Highway on the Mexican positions. The main American objective targeted the "Tete de Point," a fortified bridge across the Churubusco River. For the first time in the war, the Americans experienced trouble in coordinating their attacks. The 11th U.S., thrown in an assault east of the highway, found the advance difficult. Forced to attack through high cornfields and irrigation ditches, the regiment fell back with heavy losses. Still, the 11th and the rest of the brigade rallied, and continued to apply heavy pressure to that sector of the Mexican defenses.[7]

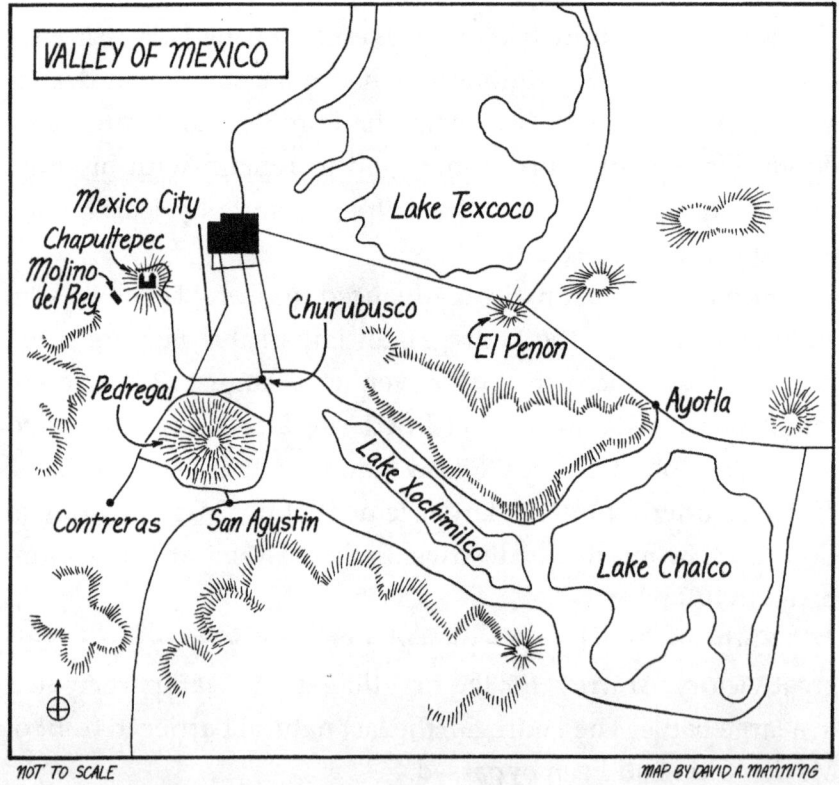

NOT TO SCALE MAP BY DAVID A. MANNING

Eventually, Scott's army drove the Mexicans from their bridge. Worth's division took the vital structure. The Americans triumphed again, but the cost had been fearsome: In a short forty-eight hours, Scott had lost 998 men, 12 percent of those engaged. The American army, and young Lieutenant William Murray, witnessed the true face of war at Churubusco.[8]

Santa Anna, with the U.S. Army only five miles from Mexico City, immediately asked for an armistice. Scott, his little army badly mauled, readily agreed. On August 24, the Tacubaya Armistice suspended the war.

Scott, even though the Mexican capital lay within his grasp, had great hopes for the Trist Mission, an effort to get Mexico to cede land by peaceful means. This proved to be a mistake. The wily Santa Anna used the respite to rebuild his shattered army and strengthen Mexico City's already formidable fortifications. When the armistice broke down upon the collapse of negotiations, this set the stage for the climactic battle for Mexico City. Scott now faced a rested enemy well over half the size of his dwindling little band.

On September 7, the armistice ended. The American army would now have to march on Mexico City. Scott had made a serious error in calling off his offense once he had the Mexican army on the run. His army would pay in blood and suffering for the precious three weeks that the Americans had unwisely given the talented Santa Anna.

During the respite, the 11th U.S. rested near Churubusco with the rest of the American army. By this time, American morale began to waver. The bloodbath at Churubusco, coupled with the task ahead, made many American soldiers uncertain of Scott's leadership. Murray nonetheless chose to stand behind his commander. During the three-week ceasefire, when Scott traveled freely among his army, Murray garnered his commanding general's attention. Within a few months, Murray found himself a close confidant of Scott's.

Despite hobnobbing in high places, Murray, like the rest of the army, realized that serious work still lay ahead. Mexico City still flaunted its heavy fortifications. The Mexican army, with a few weeks of rest and resupply, stood determined to hold the capital against the hated "gringos." Hundreds of cannon ringed the city. The task appeared impossible.

Scott did not wait long before ordering his initial assaults. The Molino del Ray, a large stone building, became Scott's first objective.[9] A nearly impregnable position, the Molino del Ray lay situated on a plain within easy cannon range of the most formidable work in Mexico City's defenses, Chapultepec Castle. General William Worth attacked the Molino in the early hours of September 8. Cadwalader's brigade remained in reserve. After advancing, Worth found himself caught in a crossfire, and his units were all but destroyed. Worth managed to seize an enemy battery, but a ferocious Mexican counterattack soon recaptured the guns and drove off the Americans. The Voltigeur Regiment and the 11th U.S. arrived to stem the tide.[10]

The two regiments succeeded in breaking into the Molino and retaking the cannon. The 11th then had to stand in the face of another fierce Mexican attack. This time the Americans held, after Murray and the rest of the 11th U.S. repulsed the Mexicans in hand-to-hand combat. The Mexican army, demoralized, fell back into the interior defenses of the capital.

The human cost had been horrific. The Americans suffered staggering losses. Seven hundred and eighty-seven men, almost a quarter of those engaged, had fallen. Daniel Harvey Hill, a young gunner with the 4th U.S. Artillery, wrote that the battle "in a great degree destroyed the confidence in our commanders." Although the American held the field, a few more such victories would use up Scott's army completely.[11]

Chapultepec still towered defiantly over the Americans. Beyond that castle stood two fortified gates. Nonetheless, Scott pushed on. Scott ordered his army to carry the castle and the two gates in one lightning strike. Scott prepared to gamble with everything he had on a single decisive blow.

Murray and his companions in the 11th suffered from exhaustion, but soldiered on. Virtually cut off from supplies, low on food and munitions, the Americans felt a growing sense of despair. Captain Hill, like many other American soldiers, felt Chapultepec to be "impregnable."[12]

Unknown to Scott, Hill, and Murray, the Mexican army lay in even worse shape than the Americans. Demoralization swept through their ranks. Despite the losses they took, the Gringos kept coming. Many Mexican soldiers, their confidence in victory waning, deserted. Mexican morale had cracked.

American artillery blasted Chapultepec all day on the 12th. That night, Scott organized his assault. He ordered Twiggs to launch a diversionary assault south of the capital. Pillow's and General John Quitman's divisions provided the real thrust from the west. At eight o'clock on September 13, the American columns rushed forward.

Colonel William B. Trousdale led his own 14th U.S. and the 11th U.S. in a special attack column east from the Molino towards the castle. Four other columns converged on the castle. As the 11th and 14th U.S. surged forward, they came under a murderous fire from Chapultepec. A section of artillery supported the 11th and 14th, commanded by a young Virginia lieutenant named Thomas Jonathan Jackson. Over a decade later, and under much different circumstances, Murray would eventually encounter this young lieutenant again.[13]

The American columns plunged through the withering Mexican fire, and threw up their scaling ladders. As the Americans surged into the castle, the Mexicans broke and either ran or surrendered. The Stars and Stripes flew over the last major bastion in front of Mexico City. Watching the appalling spectacle, one Mexican officer remarked, "God is a Yankee."[14]

The Americans, keeping up their momentum, followed up the attack. The American army, including the 11th U.S., stormed the Belen Gateway. To the north, Worth succeeded in driving the Mexicans as well. Nothing could now postpone the inevitable fall of Mexico City.

That night, Santa Anna withdrew his beaten army from the capital. The next day, Scott's triumphant army occupied the city. For Murray and most of the rest of Scott's army, the war had ended. With the American victory, the warring nations signed a peace treaty. The rest of 1847 remained pleasant for the occupying Americans. Mexico City had many charms, and the troops now relaxed after their long march and ordeal. Many American soldiers attended High Mass in Mexico City's innumerable Catholic churches. Murray, who had been raised a devout Catholic by his father, probably did the same.[15]

During this period, Murray grew increasingly closer to his commander in chief. Soon, Murray carried dispatches for Scott. Scott had become embroiled in a political dispute with Polk. Scott prepared secret dispatches to Secretary of War William Marcy. He chose William Murray to carry them back to Washington. Murray's service in Mexico had ended.[16]

After another long voyage at sea, Murray arrived back in the United States. After the delivery of Scott's dispatches in Washington, Murray—to his great chagrin—received orders to proceed to Philadelphia for recruiting duty.[17] Nonetheless, Murray obeyed, and succeeded in recruiting a sizable body of men. Afterwards, the army ordered Murray to Easton, Pennsylvania, where he again proved adept at raising volunteers. Murray's charisma and his prior military experience undoubtedly helped him ingratiate himself with potential recruits. Murray excelled in these skills, and would never lose them.[18]

Despite this success, Murray missed his regiment and comrades. He requested a transfer back into the ranks of the 11th U.S. Eventually, the War Department granted this request. Murray prepared to sail for Mexico, when he received word that his marching orders had been countermanded. Murray's skill as a recruiter had proved too valuable. Ordered to Fort McHenry, Murray trained and organized even more new recruits. He remained there until the spring of 1848, when the American army began to finally depart from Mexico.[19]

Murray next moved to Fort Hamilton, in New York harbor. Here, he assisted in discharging the troops returning from Mexico. Soon, all of the American units had returned. Murray considered staying in the army. In fact, his superiors urged him to, but he refused. His family convinced him that a businessman's life was far more lucrative than that of a soldier. Murray resigned from the army sometime in the middle of 1848. Murray's first great military experience had ended.[20]

CHAPTER 4
A Civilian Again

Murray made the transition from soldier to civilian fairly easily. The veteran twenty-three-year-old moved to Hollidaysburg, in Blair County, Pennsylvania. Murray quickly and successfully returned to the mercantile business.

Yet Murray, like most veterans, had changed in the war. He had finely honed his natural ability as a leader. Exposed to the petty squabbles that the American officer corps had engaged in during the Mexican War, Murray now showed a marked interest in politics. Although he had served under Winfield Scott—a Whig—Murray soon became a devoted Democrat. Murray quickly became a rising star in the Democratic Party in Blair County, Pennsylvania.[1]

By 1850, Murray's future seemed secure. His business thrived, as did all of Blair County. During this period, the handsome young veteran met a woman. Elizabeth, born in 1829, was the daughter of John Daugherty, the owner of the "Exchange Hotel" in Hollidaysburg. The couple's relationship blossomed, and with the approval of her father, the couple wed on July 13, 1851. Father John Walsh married the couple in St. Mary's Catholic Church in downtown Hollidaysburg.[2]

William Murray, shown here as a civilian. This image probably dates to the mid-1850s. This image is previously unpublished.

Courtesy Blair County Historical Society

The Murrays soon settled down. William took an increasingly active part in the local activities of the Democratic Party. Only a few months after the Murrays wed, Elizabeth became pregnant. On July 16, 1852, Elizabeth, assisted by midwife Catharine O'Friel, gave birth to a daughter. The Murrays christened the baby Mary Carmel.[3]

Mary Murray proved a sickly child. For most of her life, she would have serious medical problems. Likely crippled, and suffering from other "physical infirmities," Mary proved both a blessing and a burden to her parents.[4]

National issues also pressed on Murray. A dedicated Democrat, Murray supported Franklin Pierce in the presidential election of 1852. Ironically, Pierce's opponent was none other than Winfield Scott. Murray campaigned long and hard in Blair County for Pierce. Eventually, Pierce handily won the presidency.

In reward for his services, Pierce appointed William Murray to the position of postmaster of Hollidaysburg. By any definition, Murray had achieved success. Now a prominent businessman, father, and political appointee, Murray's future appeared to be secure.[5]

The Murrays continued to prosper during the next few years. In late 1853 or early 1854, Elizabeth Murray became pregnant with her second child. On August 24, 1854, Elizabeth gave birth to a healthy son, named John Bartholomew, in honor of both his parents' fathers. Murray continued to work at his duties, and became an increasingly important civic leader.[6]

Murray excelled as postmaster, and his support for the Democratic Party grew. In the Election of 1856, Murray backed James Buchanan. Buchanan won, and promptly reappointed Murray to his post. On January of 1859, Murray and Elizabeth gave birth to a third child, named Sarah Gray. Unfortunately, like Mary, Sarah proved a weak child.[7]

Divided by sectional differences, controversy tore at Buchanan's administration. The Democratic Party had difficulty in coping with national issues, such as the Panic of 1857. As the nation edged towards secession and civil war, the Democratic Party became increasingly ineffective. Murray remained loyal to his party, but remained a firm "Northern" Democrat. His loyalties lay with the Union and the state of Pennsylvania. In 1859, Murray became an officer in the "Scott Legion," a Philadelphia militia company dedicated to preserving the Union. Although an honorific title more than anything else, Murray's acceptance clearly demonstrated his sectional loyalty.[8]

By 1860, Murray's attention, like most Americans', focused on national events. Again, Murray campaigned for the Democratic Party. Then, personal tragedy struck the Murray household; Elizabeth Murray fell ill. The family called upon Dr. J. A. Landis, a local medical man. The surgeon diagnosed Elizabeth with "consumption," a pulmonary infection with no cure. At roughly the same time, young daughter Sarah died.[9]

As 1861 approached, and lights began to go out over the "United" States, Murray's attention remained on his wife. Elizabeth, saddened by the death of her youngest child, grew weaker. Even the shock of losing his post (the Republican Party had won the election of 1860) and the formation of the Confederate States of America could not separate Murray from his wife's bedside.[10]

As the Civil War began, the Federal army had a serious shortage of experienced officers. The army offered Murray a commission as a captain in the Regulars. With his wife near death, Murray refused. Even the Federal disaster at First Bull Run could not move him. On August 26, 1861, Elizabeth Murray died. Murray, heartbroken, eventually recovered enough to pursue military matters. He offered his service to his state, and did not have long to wait. In October, Governor Andrew Curtin of Pennsylvania authorized him to raise, organize, and take command of a regiment of volunteers. Murray, now a colonel, had returned to the army.[11]

While Murray prepared to depart for training camp, a letter appeared in a Hollidaysburg newspaper. The letter described the need for renewed sacrifice in the escalating conflict:

> As the war advances, the necessities of the crisis become gradually more and more apparent. The men and boys who enlisted under the influence of a mere holiday patriotism, have found out their mistake. The war, which, in the preparation, was a thing of music and parade, and gay uniforms, has dropped his merry aspect amidst the realities of the field, and it now appears in "garments rolled in blood, its face begrimed with the smoke and smut of battle"...Holiday soldiers must unlearn their early lessons, or suffer shame for their folly.
>
> ...Killing others is a work which he does in common with the hangman, but he becomes a hero, though unnamed, as soon as he sets himself up as a mark for the rifles of his enemies. Just there is the ugly reality, and yet the real glory of the romance of war...
>
> Another thing to be remembered by our soldiers in the field, and by those who enter it hereafter, is that they belong to the service until their valor shall reestablish peace...If they would be true to the soldier's oath, and successful in the strife, they must regard military discipline as a religious duty. Each individual must allow himself to be absorbed into the aggregate life of the army, must feel that he is only a part of a great vital machine, whose successful working depends on completeness of combination and facility of response to the touch of the chief engineer.
>
> ...If a man of God, a true minister, is needed anywhere, at any time, it is in the hospital after the battle,

to catch the last word of the dying, and to give in exchange the consolations of the Gospel, and if any congregation needs moral and religious training for its duties, needs to be built up, armed, equipped, with holy motives and incentives, it is a regiment gathered together on purpose to be exposed to death.

This letter, obviously written by a soldier who had seen war, appeared in the *Hollidaysburg Register*, and bore the signature "M." Only one veteran in the town possessed all of these traits: William Gray Murray. In the letter, Murray attempted to explain to his countrymen the true nature of war, and the sacrifices that their soldiers would have to endure. Many people, North and South, still believed the war would end within the year. Harsh realism, like that found in "M's" essay, proved serious stuff in the heady days of 1861.[12]

Chapter 5

The 84th Is Formed

Murray hurried into the field. He soon took charge of Camp Crossman, a training and organizational camp located three miles from Huntingdon, Pennsylvania. Murray worked hard getting the green recruits into shape. The colonel installed a rigorous "pass" system, which effectively kept the new recruits in their camps. Murray himself often rode out and greeted newly arrived greenhorns. After greeting the new soldiers, Murray supervised the distribution of blankets, tents, and camp equipment. Impressed with their new colonel's kindly nature and professional demeanor, one soldier wrote: "everybody in town (Huntingdon), camp, and country has cause to rejoice the selection made by Gen. James of Col. Murray for commander of the post."[1]

Pennsylvania assigned Murray to be the senior colonel in a special "Mountain Brigade," a proposed outfit with three regiments of foot with attached cavalry and artillery. The brigade fell under the leadership of one J. Y. James, a Democratic politician. The brigade had three proposed regiments; the 84th, under Murray; the 110th, under Colonel William Lewis; and another regiment, tentatively numbered the 39th, under Colonel Jacob Ziegler. The cavalry and artillery never materialized, and although the 84th organized, the other two regiments merged into the 110th, under Lewis. Murray took command of the 84th Pennsylvania Volunteers.²

The men of the 84th enjoyed life in Camp Crossman. "Nothing to do but eat, drink and be merry" in the words of one Pennsylvania private. The companies began to drill, and Murray attempted to established a semblance of military order.³

However, trouble brewed. Several of the 110th's companies consisted of Irishmen from Philadelphia. Many of these boys from Philadelphia, a rowdy set, had a strong fondness for alcohol. Members of the 110th regularly left the camp at night to procure booze from nearby towns. On one occasion, a soldier failed to give the correct countersign upon returning to camp and received a musket shot in the leg. Several times Colonel Murray placed drunken members of the 110th Pennsylvania under arrest and confined them to the guardhouse. Angered by Murray, a large mob of drunken members of the 110th planned to raid the camp of the 84th and "clean them out." Murray got wind of the enterprise, and set his whole regiment out, armed with clubs and shovels, to meet the raiders from the 110th. Harvey Wells, a young volunteer in the 84th, remembered that they stood ready to welcome the 110th with "bloody hands and hospitable graves." Wells also remembered—years later in jest—being "more frightened that night than ever after in any of the numerous battles and skirmishes in which the regiment participated in the next three years." The 84th repulsed the 110th, and returned to their camps in peace.⁴

The 84th continued to drill and train as November rolled in. Samuel Bryan, first lieutenant of Company B, remembered that "It is pretty cold here. We have a cook shanty made out of pine poles and pine brush and an arch over the head of our street made of hickory poles and spruce." Bryan remembered the time as "quite romantic." The war seemed far away for the men of the 84th and 110th.⁵

Back in the army again: William Murray in uniform, taken upon his commission as colonel of the 84th Pennsylvania Volunteer Infantry.

Courtesy Blair County Historical Society

In the latter part of November, the 84th relocated to Camp Curtin, near Harrisburg, in order to better prepare for actual field service. Like Camp Crossman, Curtin provided a comfortable locale. One soldier of the 84th remarked that he liked "Camp Curtin as well as Camp Crossman." The enlistments continued. By the end of November, roughly nine companies organized for service.[6]

Training continued through the first two weeks of December. On December 21, the 84th Pennsylvania formed up before the state capital at Harrisburg. Murray and the regiment prepared to receive their first flag from the state. Governor Andrew Curtin presented the flag and addressed the large crowd that turned out to watch the spectacle. After Governor Curtin finished his speech, Colonel Murray stepped forward and addressed the crowd:

> I accept this beautiful standard, presented by the Legislature of the Keystone State, through you, its honored chief magistrate, in such glowing and eloquent terms. As the period for speech making has passed, and the hour for energetic action has arrived, my remarks on this occasion shall be brief, as becomes a soldier. In accepting this flag on behalf of the regiment, I do with full consciousness of the relation which both officers and men bear to our noble state, and the nation whose cause we have espoused. Permit me to thank you sir, for the terms of commendation in which you have pleased to speak of the 84th, and of my humble self, and to assure you that whatever our fate may be in the future, we will endeavor by good conduct, and a strict discharge of our duties, to make such a record as will bring no dishonor upon the Stars and Stripes, which we go to maintain and defend, or the

The 84th Is Formed

proud Commonwealth whose sons we deem it an honor to call ourselves.

Murray followed his little speech with a bit of doggerel:

> *No Shrewish tears shall fill our eyes,*
> *When the sword hilts in our hand;*
> *Heart whole we'll part and not a sigh*
> *For the fairest in the land.*
> *Let piping swain and craven wight*
> *Thus weep and pulling cry;*
> *our business is like men to fight,*
> *And hero like to die.*[7]

After finishing his little inspirational to the crowd, Murray stepped forward and delivered the colors into the hand of Color Sergeant Ned Stokes. "Into your hands I entrust this standard. Answer for its safety with your life." Stokes answered: "Governor and Colonel: If I don't return this flag, 'twill be because Ned Stokes will occupy five feet of ground."[8] Two days later, the 84th officially mustered into the service of the United States.

The 84th had only nine companies, A, B, C, D, E, F, G, I, and K, when it mustered in. Company H had not yet formed. The total strength of the 84th was 766 officers and men. A few men, like Darsey Houck, first sergeant of Company E, had seen action in the Mexican War. Unfortunately, the vast majority of the 84th's men, although considered of "good quality," had never before heard a shot fired in anger.[9]

The lieutenant colonel of the 84th was Thomas C. MacDowell, a prominent Democratic politician and editor of the *Harrisburg Patriot*. MacDowell, although an influential citizen, had no formal military experience. The major of the regiment, Walter Barrett, a lawyer and son of a powerful state judge, also lacked military training. Barrett also had a fondness for the bottle. Most of the company officers also lacked military experience. The 84th's adjutant, Thomas H. Craig, had been a business associate of Murray's, and owed his appointment solely to his relationship with his colonel. For all of his admirable qualities, Murray practiced favoritism.[10]

The 84th continued to drill during the last week in December, the soldiers spending their first Christmas away from home. The regiment still lacked arms, so some training, such as bayonet drill, proved nearly impossible. Unknown to the 84th, the week proved to be the last one of peace the regiment would enjoy for nearly four years.

On New Year's Eve the 84th received urgent orders to proceed immediately to the front, even though the men still lacked muskets. The move, completely unexpected by Murray and the regiment, started about 2:00 p.m. The 84th boarded the Cumberland Valley Railroad at the Harrisburg Depot. That evening, they set out for Hagerstown, Maryland. Early on the first day of 1862, the 84th fell in, and began their first forced march. Their destination: Hancock, Maryland.[11]

CHAPTER 6

Hancock

No survivor in the 84th's ranks on January 1, 1862, ever forgot that first march. Several inches of snow already covered the ground. Driving snow and icy winds battered the rookies of the 84th. The men, still unused to their packs, struggled to keep up with the pace of the march. To keep their spirits up, the men sang "Oh, Johnny! Why did You Go for a Soldier Boy." Harvey Wells remembered the "agony of blistered feet, stiffened joints, and ravenous stomachs." Soon after dark, the 84th camped out in the open, near Clear Spring, Maryland. The Pennsylvanians lacked tents, and slept on the snow-covered ground. Murray rested with his men, equally exposed to the elements. The 84th's introduction to army life, especially in light of the comforts of Camp Crossman and Curtin, harshly introduced the novices to soldiering in the Civil War.[1]

Few men in the regiment slept at all that brutal night. At first light, the men fell in, and continued the march for Hancock, by way of the National Pike. One soldier of the 84th claimed "the country through which we marched was rather rough, and the appearance of things in general, was not calculated to impress one very favorably with the institution of slavery. The villages through which we passed (characteristic of the South), are rather somber and dilapidated looking places." Around noon, the 84th entered the sleepy little Maryland village.[2]

Hancock, a tiny settlement along the north bank of the Potomac River, lay surrounded by high ground. A ferry ran between the banks of the Potomac. Hancock had but a single main street, which ran along the Chesapeake and Ohio Canal. From the high ground above the town the men of the 84th could clearly see Virginia, the land of the enemy.

Across the Potomac, a few companies of the 39th Illinois guarded the Baltimore and Ohio Railroad. A large Confederate force under Thomas Jonathan "Stonewall" Jackson threatened the vital railroad. The rail line had to be secured.

The 84th set up quarters in an area recently occupied by the men of the 13th Massachusetts. Unlike the previous night, the soldiers did not lack for decent quarters. Two full companies of the 84th spent the night of January 2 in a schoolhouse. Another company slept in a public house named the "Fair View Inn." Still without arms, the 84th rested following their ordeal the previous day.[3]

The next day the regiment fell in and prepared to finally receive their muskets. A shipment of arms waited in storage in Hancock, and Murray ordered the muskets distributed to his men. Unfortunately, the quality of the muskets proved to be very poor. Made in Belgium, the .69 caliber rifled muskets lacked accuracy, and weighed a cumbersome nine pounds. The United States, desperate for any weapons to suppress the rebellion, ordered thousands of these substandard muskets at the outbreak of the conflict.

To make matters worse, the Belgian muskets had to be unpacked from their shipping crates. Upon opening the crates, the men of the 84th discovered the weapons caked with tallow, and in need of adjustment. The men had to clean the rifles before they

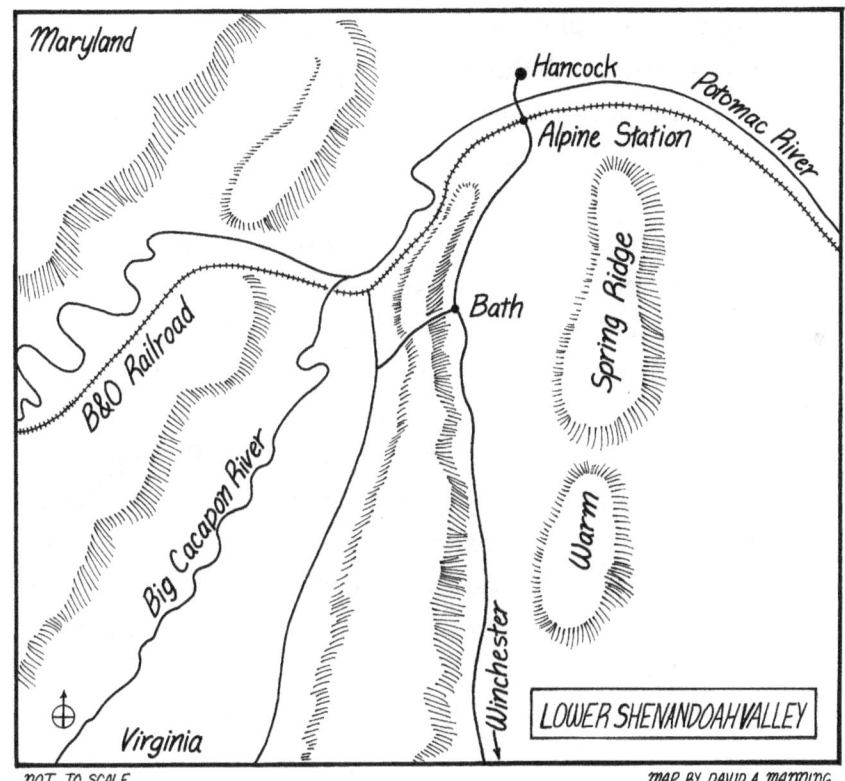

MAP BY DAVID A. MANNING

became serviceable. Nonetheless, eager for any weapons, the raw recruits of the 84th were still "well pleased," in the words of one private.[4]

While his men worked on their guns, Colonel Murray received an urgent dispatch from Bath, six miles south of the Potomac. A section of the 39th Illinois, supported by two guns, ran into some Confederate pickets, six more miles south of Bath. While most of the green 39th held their position, a few men panicked, and ran back to the ferry.

Two men with the 39th Illinois, recently ferried back from the Virginia side, burst into Murray's headquarters. After locating Murray, the two men wove a tale of disaster, claiming that the 39th had been "cut to pieces." Soon after, Dr. Samuel Blake, also with the 39th, arrived at Murray's headquarters, and reported to Murray a more accurate and detailed account of what had transpired that afternoon. Although sorely pressed, the 39th still held its ground. A relieved Murray told Dr. Blake that the previous two men "acted as if they were crazy; I could get no definite idea of what had occurred, or where it had occurred, or by whose orders they were sent to me." Murray promised to come to the support of the beleaguered 39th Illinois.[5]

At 10:00 p.m., Murray formed his regiment in the streets of Hancock and ordered it to cross the Potomac. Using a large "flat," or ferry, eight companies crossed the freezing Potomac. Company F remained behind to guard Hancock. One Pennsylvanian remembered: "the night was exceedingly stormy, the snow and sleet falling fast, and the fire on each side of the river, to guide the ferryman, gave to the scene a truly romantic appearance, reminding one of the crossing of the Delaware by the immortal Washington."[6]

As soon as his companies finished crossing, Murray met with Lieutenant Colonel Thomas Osborn of the 39th Illinois at Alpine Station, directly across the river from Hancock. Osborn reported to Murray that the real fight lay to the south, at Bath. Earlier in the day, a small detachment of the 39th had ambushed and killed a few members of Turner Ashby's Confederate cavalry. The Rebels then brought up several regiments of infantry as reinforcements. By remaining at Bath and the south side of the Potomac, the 39th Illinois risked immediate destruction or capture.[7]

Murray immediately ordered his regiment to fall in, and personally led the 84th down the North Road towards Bath. Murray and his regiment arrived at their destination around midnight. The exhausted men immediately bedded down for the night, taking shelter in the tiny village's few houses. Murray, meanwhile, held a council of war with Major Orrin Mann of the 39th Illinois and Lieutenant E. D. Muhlenburg, commander of a section of artillery from Battery K, 4th U.S. Artillery. The three officers decided to hold their position overlooking the town until morning.[8]

The exhausted 84th had only a few hours to enjoy their brief respite. As Murray conversed with his fellow officers, some local Unionist Virginians came into the camp and informed the colonel that Thomas "Stonewall" Jackson, with some nine thousand men, was approaching the town. Murray and his small command, outnumbered by ten to one, lay in great danger.[9]

Murray planned to eventually fall back, but not without first making a stand. Sometime between four and five o'clock, the 84th's officers roused their men and passed the word to fall in. The 84th marched up the steep sides of Warm Spring Ridge, a "mountain" that overlooked the town.[10] Muhlenburg put his two guns into position, and Major Mann prepared the men of the 39th Illinois. A small squadron of Pennsylvania cavalry, under the command of a Lieutenant Patterson, mounted.[11]

The tiny Union brigade finished deploying and prepared for battle. They did not have long to wait. At around 9:00 a.m., Confederate cavalry appeared in Murray's front.[12]

Murray now faced a major dilemma: his regiment's Belgian muskets were still by and large unserviceable. Fortunately, the 39th Illinois had excellent new Springfield Model 1861 Rifle Muskets. The colonel ordered the 39th forward, and held his own regiment in reserve. Murray also received a dispatch from Cumberland, stating that the 13th Indiana Infantry would soon arrive in support.[13]

Murray deployed Companies A, B, and C of the 84th to the right, along Warm Spring Ridge. Companies K and I fell in to the left. Company E, the largest, waited in reserve.[14] Lieutenant Jonathan Derno, of Company A, led a small patrol from the ridge to scout out the advancing Confederate horsemen. Murray ordered another reconnaissance, the little cavalry command, to the front. Surgeon Gideon Hoop of the 84th accompanied this tiny band of horsemen.[15]

Derno soon brought his command back into the Union lines. The young lieutenant immediately reported that beyond the Confederate cavalry lay a large contingent of Confederate infantry. At roughly the same time, Patterson's Yankee cavalry returned at a gallop. Like Derno's men, they had run into a body of Confederate infantry. After sustaining a volley which dismounted seven men, Patterson's cavalry returned to the main Federal line like "thunder rolling up a hill side." As Surgeon Hoop returned, his horse bucked wildly. Seeing this, Muhlenburg's gunners gave Hoop a cheer. When the breathless doctor returned, Murray asked him why he undertook so great a risk by accompanying the small patrol. Hoop replied, "Why Sir, I trusted in god and Lieutenant Muhlenburg's Parrott gun!"[16]

Patterson, Derno, and Hoop confirmed Murray's fears: the small Federal command risked immediate destruction if it attempted to hold its ground. The large Confederate force overlapped both Murray's flanks, and advanced by way of the Martinsburg Pike, thus threatening the Federals' line of retreat. Reluctantly, Murray ordered his little brigade to fall back to Hancock.[17]

Noiselessly, the 84th pulled off Warm Spring Ridge, and began a long and dangerous march back to the Potomac River. Murray ordered his men to retire by way of the North Road, which ran parallel to Sir John's Run. Company I of the 84th fanned out to protect the small Federal column. The section of infantry from the 39th Illinois also deployed as skirmishers, and covered Murray's exposed flanks. Muhlenburg pushed his limbered guns along the North Road as well. The artillery pieces severely slowed the column. When an officer suggested to Murray that it might be impossible to rescue the two cannon, Murray replied: "Sir, it must be done!"[18]

Murray's main column, meanwhile, had reached the banks of the Potomac, near the conflux of Sir John's Run. The baggage train, Muhlenburg's guns, and Murray's servant crossed.[19] To Murray's relief, he discovered the 13th Indiana, recently arrived by train. Relief turned to disgust when Murray learned that the Hoosiers lacked ammunition. Helpless, the 13th quickly reboarded their train, and rode back to Cumberland. Murray's small command, with not enough trains to carry them, followed the tracks back to the ferry.[20]

The Union column marched through the afternoon. Around dusk, the exhausted Yankees reached Alpine Station, across the river from Hancock. Turner Ashby's ubiquitous Confederate cavalry already lapped at the rear of Murray' troops. Murray immediately ordered the three companies of the 39th Illinois into line, supported by Company I of the 84th. The small command rushed to engage the Confederates pushing up from the rear.

As the cavalry troopers of Ashby's 7th Virginia advanced, they spotted the Federals to their front, about a quarter of a mile from Alpine Station. Immediately, the Virginians sounded the charge and surged forward to engage the hated Yankees. As the Confederate cavalry closed in on the Federal lines, they received several volleys from the three companies of the 39th Illinois and Company I of the 84th. Thirteen Rebel cavalryman fell, including a lieutenant.[21]

Murray's main body at Alpine Station could see the welcome campfires of Company F in Hancock. The men began to board the ferries in order to cross the river, but progress proved slow. The Confederates brought up a few cannon and began an artillery barrage. Some of the green troops of the 84th, their nerves already stretched to the breaking point by their recent ordeal, panicked and attempted to risk the frigid waters of the Potomac. One private, Theodore Pardee of Hillsdale, Pennsylvania, drowned. Poor Pardee had the dubious distinction of being the first fatality the 84th suffered in the war.[22]

Murray addressed his men, and attempted to calm the wavering troops of the 84th. Corporal Read, of Company I, captured the spirit, if not the actual letter, of Murray's speech in a note home: "Fellow soldiers! You are on the bank of the river and the enemy is in your rear and may attack you before you get over, but if he does, give him hell! Stand right up to him, fight men, and die like soldiers. You have but once to die, for if you undertake to wade, there will be the half, if not all of you drowned!"[23]

Eventually, Murray calmed the retreating Yankee column sufficiently to begin an orderly crossing of the Potomac. A few lucky men crossed on the ferry. Several more unfortunate soldiers had to wade the freezing waters of the Potomac.

Despite the artillery fire and the loss of Private Pardee, the rest of Murray's small command crossed safely. Company E acted as the rear guard. Major Barrett, bringing up the rear, rode into the river, the last man to cross. While in midstream, he rescued an exhausted Patrick Gallagher, the captain of Company E, who had slipped and begun sinking into the river.[24]

Even before the 84th had finished crossing, the town of Hancock had already fallen under artillery fire. Muhlenburg, having returned to Hancock, swiftly brought up his guns. Muhlenburg deployed his guns on the high ground north of Hancock and began to return fire. Many of the citizens of the town, terrified by the cannonade, fled. Soon, the Rebels' guns fell silent, except for an occasional shot.[25]

At this point, Murray formed up the 84th, as well as his detachment of the 39th Illinois. Murray told the assembled men that "he would never surrender," and that he "desired them to stick to him until there was not a man left." To this stirring address, the men of the 84th and the 39th responded enthusiastically.[26]

As Colonel Murray spoke to his men, a large body of Confederate infantry appeared on the high ground across from Hancock. Anxious moments passed. At midnight, the tiny garrison saw a welcome sight: the 110th Pennsylvania, just arrived from Camp Curtin. The 110th, like the 84th, had not been issued arms prior to their arrival at Hancock. Unlike the 84th, the 110th already suffered from demoralization. During the march to Hancock, a riot had broken out between the Philadelphians and the boys from western Pennsylvania. Several men were killed, and many more wounded. The 110th, still a rabble, was even less prepared for a fight than the 84th.[27]

Well after midnight, General Frederick West Lander, Murray's division commander, arrived from Williamsport. Lander had spent nearly the entire day in the saddle, having left Hagerstown as soon as he had been informed about the action near Bath. Lander located Murray as soon as he arrived. After Murray informed the general of the situation, Lander ordered the infantry deployed in the streets of Hancock, thus shielding them from the occasional Confederate cannonballs that streaked through the cold January night.[28]

The following morning, a body of Confederate horsemen appeared opposite Hancock, at Alpine Station. The Confederate cavalrymen carried a flag of truce, and requested an audience with the Union commander. The Federals requisitioned the ferry, and brought over a single Rebel officer. This officer proved to be none other than Lieutenant Colonel Turner Ashby, Jackson's able chief of cavalry. General Lander dispatched William Murray to ascertain what Ashby wanted and if need be to bring the Confederate officer to his headquarters.

Ashby, ever the bold cavalier, came to the point at once. He urged Murray to "stack arms" and surrender within two hours, or an artillery barrage would again fall on the town. Not intimidated, Murray replied that he had "some men here who intended to fight until the last one falls, and if you undertake to cross you will have to run your own risk." Murray then had the Confederate cavalryman blindfolded, and escorted him to Lander's headquarters.[29]

Lander located his headquarters in the town telegraph office. Murray brought Ashby into the room where Lander and Major Orrin Mann nervously waited for transmissions. Fearing that Ashby might understand the incoming messages, Lander ordered the blindfolded Confederate brought into another room. After the Federals removed Ashby's blindfold, the cocky cavalryman handed Lander a dispatch from Jackson demanding the town's surrender. Lander read the dispatch, and snapped, "Colonel Ashby, give my compliments to General Jackson and tell him to bombard and be damned! If he opens his batteries on this town he will injure more of his friends than he will of the enemy, for this is a damned secesh place, anyhow." Ashby sat up to depart. Lander, after having thought about his previous reply, said: "Hold it! Take a seat, Colonel Ashby. General Jackson has addressed me in a polite and soldierly manner and it demands a like reply. I take back all that I have said and will write what I have to communicate." Lander wrote a brief refusal to Jackson, and told Ashby as he departed, "General Jackson and yourself, Colonel Ashby, are gentlemen and brave men, without a question, but you are started out on a damned bad cause." Lander then shook hands with Ashby before the C.S. officer, again blindfolded, departed. Murray escorted the Confederate cavalryman back to the ferry. As Ashby boarded the skiff, Murray called out to the Confederate: "We'll meet you in Dixie."[30]

Like Murray earlier, Lander next rode among the Federal regiments and praised the men. As General Lander approached the 84th, he called out: "Soldiers, do your duty! There is work for you today; if I am killed, someone else will take my place."[31]

That night, after a few brief artillery salvoes, the Confederates withdrew. All through the day, Murray walked among his regiment and praised his men, calling the soldiers his "bushwhackers." Hancock and its tiny garrison, due in no small part to Murray's tenacity and courage, had been saved. Later, General Lander would say of Murray's determined stand and retreat, "If he was not a military man it did honor to his genius."[32]

Murray had indeed pulled off one of the most remarkable coups in the early part of the Civil War. With fewer than one thousand men, Murray had successfully bamboozled and escaped some nine thousand Confederate troops under the direct leadership of the great "Stonewall" Jackson. Murray had not only called Jackson's bluff by making a stand, he successfully retreated his command in the face of crack Confederate cavalry and overwhelming numbers. Hancock, with its vital supplies and proximity to the strategically important Baltimore and Ohio Railroad, remained securely in Federal hands. Although small, the affairs at Bath and Hancock proved vital in stopping Jackson's Winter Campaign. Murray's escape from Bath and the affair at Hancock proved to be the high point of his military career in the Civil War.

Chapter 7
Winter Activities

The 84th remained in Hancock until January 10, 1862. For the most part, the time passed uneventfully. A few new men arrived to join the 84th, mostly late recruits who missed the regiment's departure from Camp Curtin. The 84th kept themselves busy preparing their Belgian muskets for use.

At 6:45 on January 10, the 84th finally received new marching orders. The 84th, accompanied by the 110th Pennsylvania, started on a forced march to Cumberland, Maryland. Murray rode well ahead of his men in order to secure decent lodgings for his regiment.

Like their first march from Pennsylvania, the 84th again suffered greatly. The men made eighteen miles that day, then bedded down for the night. Early the next morning, the two regiments resumed their march.

During the next day's march, Major Barrett and Colonel William Lewis of the 110th became quite drunk while riding alongside their infantry. The two inebriated officers decided to hold a race between the two Pennsylvania outfits. Both officers rode among their men and beseeched them not to let the other regiment win. Eventually, the two regiments became blended into one, and by the time they reached Cumberland, twenty-two miles away, all semblance of organization had vanished. In the words of Harvey Wells, it "was big fun for those two officers on horseback, to witness a race between the two regiments, the men not yet used to carrying guns and accoutrements, and handicapped with knapsacks as large as a Saratoga Trunk." Wells continued, "it was one of those foolish things done in the army and had its incentive in the whiskey carried by the men on horseback." Stragglers from both regiments continued to trickle into Cumberland for five days after the march.[1]

On January 13, the 84th reported to Colonel Nathan Kimball for assignment to his brigade. For the first time in the war, the 84th officially became part of a larger organization. The 84th joined ranks with the 7th Virginia (loyal), and the 13th and 14th Indiana. The unit's baggage followed by boat.

On January 16, the 84th established a new base at Camp Kelley, some six miles downriver from Cumberland, in Virginia. For the next week, the 84th remained in camp. Company D moved briefly back to Cumberland in order to repair several defective muskets that had been issued to the company.[2]

On January 25, the 84th finally mustered for pay. The regiment had not been paid since their enlistment the previous year, and many of the unit's soldiers lacked money. To the regiment's disgust, the army had not scheduled the promised monies until the next week. While in Cumberland, Murray became ill with a violent attack of "Inflammatory Rheumatism," and had to be confined to a hospital bed.[3]

On February 5, the 84th drew pay for the first time. Even this proved a problem. Most of the soldiers expected to be paid for their entire length of service, in many cases dating back to September or October of 1861. The army decided that it owed monies only from December, the date of the 84th's acceptance into Federal service. The entire episode left a bad taste in the mouths of the men.[4]

The 84th did receive some good news, however. Murray returned, after having spent only a few days in his hospital bed. One soldier, glad to see his colonel, wrote: "Murray's arrival at camp was hailed with delight, his men are greatly attached to him. Where ever he goes they will follow, and he does not ask them to go anywhere he will not lead." Murray's popularity with the rank and file, already high, soared.[5]

The next day, Murray ordered the 84th to cook three days' rations and to prepare for a short march. At 6:00 a.m. the brigade boarded trains and rode into Oldtown, Maryland. After they arrived, the brigade marched to South Branch Bridge. The view impressed the men of the 84th. One soldier described the bridge as a "magnificent structure." The weather pounded the men with storms. Another soldier complained of the endless mud. "Mud is the all important topic with the soldiers, and the question is being seriously considered as to whether we had not better practice the art of swimming if it gets much deeper..." The 84th created temporary shelters with brush and fence rails.[6]

The regiment soon continued their winter marching. By February 9, the 84th had reached Paw Paw, a town in Virginia. One overzealous — and hungry — member of the 84th shot and slaughtered some stray animal. Unfortunately for the reputation of the regiment, Nathan Kimball witnessed the little act of vandalism. Outraged, Colonel Kimball ordered Murray to place the offending private under arrest. On the 10th, the 84th put up tents along the Potomac, and established a new camp, this one called Camp Chase. On the 11th, Kimball personally reviewed the regiment, no doubt with the animal incident in mind.[7]

Two days later, other units of Lander's division won a victory at Bloomery Gap. Although a small affair, the triumph sent morale soaring. On February 21, the 84th went through the motions of battalion drill, an exercise designed to teach the new recruits the fine art of fighting as a compact unit.

In this, the 84th sadly fell behind the other units of the brigade, the 110th excepted. This oversight proved Murray's responsibility. Murray remembered his experiences in the Mexican War. He hated the petty tyranny of army life. Murray always remembered what the common soldier had to endure, and sought not to overly trouble or strain his troops. As a result of this pampering, the 84th remained an undisciplined unit. His enlisted men may have loved him, but the 84th's development as a effective regiment lagged. The officers of the 84th increasingly resented the 84th's lack of discipline, and began to openly question Murray's leadership.

On the last day of February, the regiment mustered again for pay and received orders to move. No marching orders came, so the regiment "slept on their arms for three days." On March 2, Murray and his men received word that General Lander had died of fever. The next day, the whole outfit fell out to participate in a parade to honor the fallen captain.[8]

CHAPTER 8
Trouble at Winchester

On March 6, the 84th left for Winchester. By March 7, the 84th had reached Martinsburg, due north of Winchester. Again, the men endured a severe march.[1]

Unbeknownst to Murray, his officers' resentment had by this time boiled over. A contingent of officers, led by Captain Robert Horrell, began work on a secret document. This document called for Murray's resignation. The disgruntled officers sent the letter to Governor Curtin, and next planned to deliver the explosive missive to their colonel. Also included in the officers' request was the resignation of Major Barrett who like Murray, had drawn the ire of most of the 84th's Company commanders.

Meanwhile, the Federal units in Virginia reorganized into five new army corps. Lander's old division, now under the command of feisty Irish General James Shields, became part of Nathaniel Banks' V Corps. Banks promptly put his corps in motion, advancing on Winchester. On March 11, the 84th and the rest of Kimball's brigade reached Bunker Hill, just north of Winchester. That night, his position untenable, Stonewall Jackson withdrew from the strategic Virginia town.[2]

From March 13 to the 17, the 84th remained at Camp Kimball, two miles north of Winchester. To the regiment's resentment, the army's brass allowed no entry into the famous

Rebel town. Despite this setback, the regiment spent the time idly, except for a few daring souls who sneaked out to see Winchester. The 84th resented the fact that other elements of Banks' corps occupied the town. One member of the 84th wrote that Banks' soldiers "paraded the streets in white gloves, white shirts, and boots blackened to looking glass perfection; upon my word it makes us laugh....Is it any wonder that we laugh at these polished, powdered jacks?" Murray remained blissfully unaware of the circular moving among his officer corps.[3]

On March 18 the 84th, minus Company K, marched about eleven miles toward Strasburg, south of Winchester. The weather remained frightful, and high winds buffeted the troops. Many felt the march to be as severe as the earlier march to Hancock. The march proved too much for some. That evening, John Maloney — a lieutenant in Company E — resigned his commission for health reasons. Murray recommended the "immediate acceptance" of the resignation.[4]

Early on the nineteenth, the regiment continued on towards Strasburg. The regiment marched about one mile when they again ran into pickets of Turner Ashby's ubiquitous Rebel cavalry. A sharp skirmish ensued, and artillery fire drove off Ashby's troopers. Fortunately there were no Union casualties. On the twentieth, the 84th retraced their steps, tramping back some twenty-two miles to Camp Kimball. The exhausted 84th arrived at their tents around 8:00 p.m.[5]

Murray awoke early on the twenty-first, and sat in his tent working on administrative details. An unknown officer, probably Captain Horrell, arrived at his tent sometime during the day. The officer saluted the colonel, and handed him a letter. Upon opening the document, Murray read the contents with growing horror.

> Though it is painful yet duty, owed alike to our country and the men of the regiment, compels us, Officers of the Line, to address you on the subject of your

resignation, it is the opinion of the undersigned that though endowed with many traits which distinguish in civil life, you have yet failed to discover that peculiar genius which qualifies for martial command. To have in charge the lives, interests, and proud hopes of a regiment of patriotic and noble hearted men is a responsibility of so great moment that no one but he who is competent should assume or retain it. The conduct of the regiment since its organization has been, it is respectfully submitted, not only unsatisfactory but criminal. Lives are not to be imperiled wantonly because of inefficiency ascribable to the incompetency of command...

Believing that your pride as a high...gentleman will induce you to regard the wishes of your officers and men. It is respectfully asked that you resign your position as Colonel of the 84th Regiment of Pennsylvania Volunteers.

The request bore the signatures of seventeen line officers.[6]

Murray's world crashed down upon him. Although a very successful man, Murray had always taken great pride in his ability as a soldier. Now, his junior officers had requested his resignation. One disgruntled young lieutenant wrote his father the same day, complaining that Murray and Major Barrett, who had also received his similar letter, had proven themselves "completely incompetent." The fact that few of the dissatisfied officers had any real experience in military matters prior to 1861 must have seemed ironic to Murray. Murray steeled himself, and refused his officers' request.[7]

In truth, Murray had failed in some aspects as a commander. His regiment's discipline and drill still lagged behind the other regiments in Shields' division, the pathetic 110th Pennsylvania excepted. Back in January, General Alpheus Williams, in command of the Hancock area, thought the 84th and the 110th to be "mob" like, and "was but too glad to get rid" of them when they departed. Nonetheless, the rank and file of the 84th continued to hold their colonel in very high esteem. Many soldiers continued to praise Murray in letters to newspapers or home. A deep bond had formed between Murray and his enlisted men. Unfortunately, affection alone did not make a regiment effective. As events would soon show, Murray and his officers had little time for squabbling.[8]

Chapter 9
Kernstown

Dawn broke like any other day on Saturday, March 22, 1862. Kimball kept Murray busy by ordering the Pennsylvania colonel to detach elements of his regiment for guard duty in nearby towns. In a fit of pique, Murray ordered his officers to "drill their companies each day in company drill for two hours. Captains when fit and present for duty will be required to drill their companies personally. Strict compliance with this order will be required." Obviously, Murray intended to hold his company officers to the same standards that they found lacking in him.[1]

The rest of the regiment lounged about in their tents, awaiting drill and dinner. The various detached soldiers left for their destinations. By midday, an unexpected sound startled the soldiers of the 84th: gunfire to the south.

Orders soon arrived. General Shields had run into Confederate cavalry just south of Winchester, near the tiny hamlet of Kernstown. At around 4:30 p.m., Murray ordered eight of his nine companies to fall in and proceed to the sound of the guns. Company I remained behind to guard the 84th's camps. Eighteen-year-old Private William Gallagher, of Company E, wrote:

> ...we was in our tents as usual not thinking of anything when all at once we got orders to pack knapsacks

an be ready to fall in line in a minuets warning. But before wee could get packed we got orders to fall in. Some had knapsacks and some had none, some had haversacks and some had none, some had little pervasion and some had none, some had blankets, and some had none. So we all fell in good order and started on the double quick an all yeled like tigers.[2]

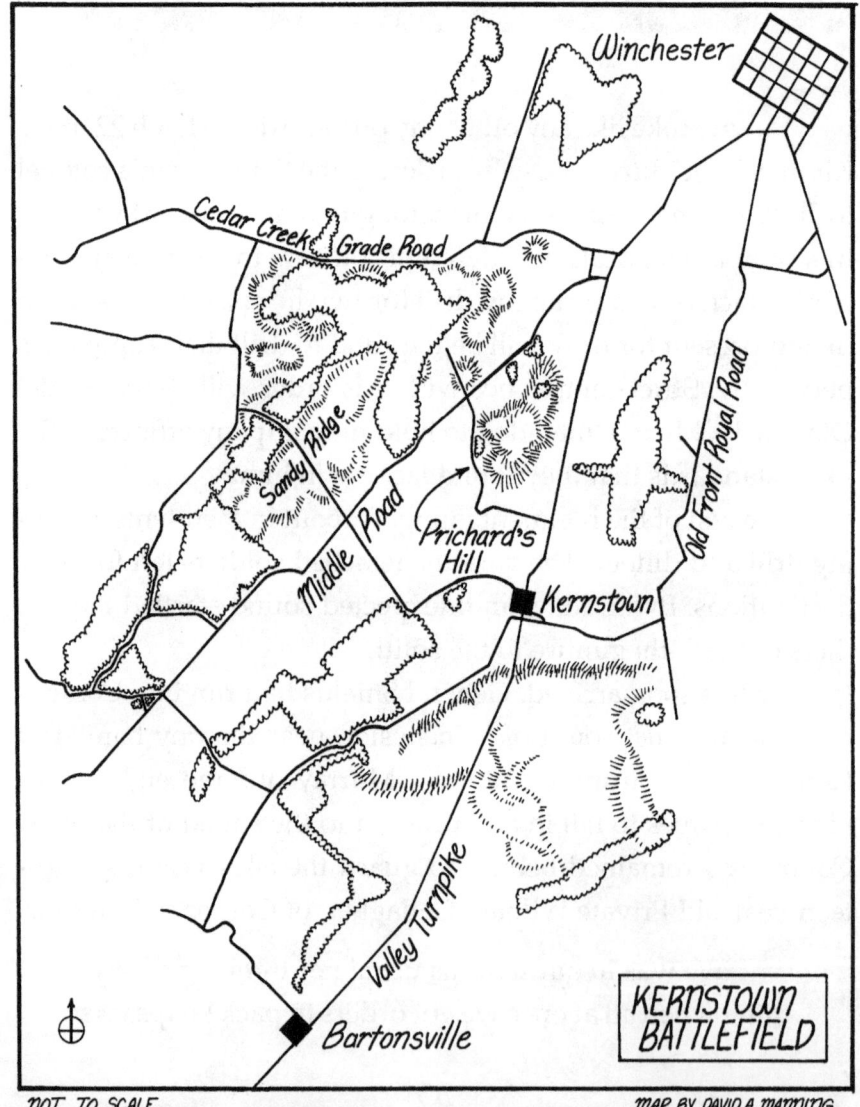

The 84th rushed down the Valley Pike for about three miles until they arrived at a large knoll named Pritchard's Hill, just north of Kernstown. There, the 84th found the rest of Kimball's brigade and two batteries of artillery, as well as another brigade of infantry under the command of Jeremiah Sullivan. Kimball's brigade sat on and around Pritchard's Hill, with the two artillery batteries. Sullivan's troops had been deployed in the fields to the east of Pritchard's Hill, astride the Valley Pike and north of Kernstown.[3]

The Federals had engaged elements of Ashby's 7th Virginia Cavalry. Ashby's troopers had a battery of artillery in support, and throughout the morning the two sides engaged in an artillery duel. Night eventually brought an end to the artillery exchange. Although the Confederates forced in Sullivan's and Kimball's pickets, they had inflicted few casualties. During this action, a shell fragment struck and severely wounded General Shields in the arm. As the day's fighting ceased, Shields rode an ambulance back into Winchester. Nathan Kimball now took command of all Federal forces in the Kernstown area.

That night, the 84th bivouacked in a cornfield adjacent to Pritchard's Hill. At first light, the sporadic skirmish fire with Ashby's troopers resumed. This action continued until around 3:00 p.m. During the interval, Corps Commander Nathaniel Banks rode into Winchester to confer with General Shields. Although both generals could hear the sounds of gunfire to the south, they concluded the action to be nothing more than skirmishing. Events would soon prove them wrong.

At 3:00 p.m., Rebel infantry appeared in the Federal front in the fields just east of Kernstown. Two Confederate infantry regiments marched forward to threaten the Union position on Pritchard's Hill. Kimball quickly shifted his brigade to meet the Confederates. Confederate artillery began to blast the hill as well. The 8th Ohio, supported by the two batteries, repulsed this first rather feeble Confederate effort. Kimball ordered the 84th to fall in and prepare to support the batteries. Private William Gallagher, of Company E, wrote: "...we got orders to fall in & we did in a minutes notice because we was all anxious for a fight. We got ordered to the front to siport the front batery of our artilery."[4]

Unbeknown to Kimball and the rest of the Federal command, Stonewall Jackson had brought up his entire little army. After being stymied in his attempt to take Pritchard's Hill, Jackson shifted his troops to his left, occupying a forested hill known as Sandy Ridge. Private Gallagher and his anxious friends would soon get their fight.

Jackson's men took Sandy Ridge with no opposition. Confederate artillery deployed on the southern end of the ridge, and began to lob shells on Pritchard's Hill. In order to counter this move, Kimball ordered Erastus Tyler's brigade, deployed north of the hill, to move and engage the Rebels on Sandy Ridge and take the Confederate batteries. All the while a fierce artillery duel raged between the two Yankee batteries on Pritchard's Hill and Jackson's guns. The Rebel shells tore up the ground on Pritchard's Hill equal to any "Bull Plough," according to young William Gallagher.[5]

Tyler's attack, poorly deployed, soon stalled. A brutal firefight raged on the north face of Sandy Ridge. Most of Jackson's three brigades defended a stonewall that ran north along the ridge. Kimball immediately realized that his brigade lay in a perfect position to threaten the Confederate right. Sullivan, with only a small body of Confederate cavalry to his front, could also be called on for support. The Rebel batteries on Sandy Ridge continued to shell Pritchard's Hill. Kimball's batteries, which had been firing at the Confederates all day, began to run low on ammunition. Kimball, his options running out, promptly ordered his brigade to attack and clear out the pesky Confederate cannon.[6]

The 67th and 8th Ohio, supported by Kimball's own 14th Indiana, became the first Union troops from Kimball's brigade to engage the Rebels. In a fierce, close range fight, the two Buckeye regiments made little headway against the Confederates in their front. The 5th Ohio and the 84th next moved out in support.

Before leaving Pritchard's Hill, Murray held a brief exchange with Kimball's artillery chief, Lieutenant Colonel Philip Daum, asking for support. At this point the 84th remained in a very exposed position, and a shell fragment soon disabled one private. Murray, resplendent in his uniform and riding a large charger, rode to his men and gave the command "attention!" The 84th quickly fell in. Murray addressed his regiment briefly, asking them to "remember the beautiful ladies of Harrisburg" and the flag which they had bestowed on the regiment. Murray next ordered his men to "right face — right shoulder shift arms — file left — double-quick — march!" The 84th stepped out smartly, and prepared to enter their first real battle.[7]

Murray had much to worry about. His men had substandard weapons, and Company I — despite being ordered up — had not rejoined the regiment. Detachments and hard service had now whittled Murray's strength down to about 255 men. Still, even with this small force, Murray prepared to charge a Rebel battery to his front, some six hundred yards off. Nonetheless, Murray threw himself into the task with speed and dedication. For the first time since Hancock, Murray was in his element. Now came the chance to prove to his upstart amateur officers his true mettle. Murray steeled himself and his regiment for the coming storm.[8]

The 84th moved out smartly, the soldiers yelling with enthusiasm. Private William Gallagher remembered the yell as "equel to anny canon" in noise. The 84th descended the hill, made two oblique turns, and moved into the woods at the base of Sandy Ridge. Meanwhile, the other engaged regiments of

Chapter 9

Kimball's brigade brought the battle to a crescendo. To the right of the 84th, the 14th Indiana had come in behind the 5th Ohio, and had begun firing into the Confederate lines. Some of the 14th Indiana's musket fire struck the rear of the 5th Ohio, who began to shout back at the Hoosiers: "quit firing! You are firing into your own men!"

The Southern troops to the right of the 5th Ohio, two companies of the 1st Virginia Battalion, heard this desperate shout. Soon a new Yankee regiment approached their front, the 84th Pennsylvania. The 84th managed to get off a few ragged volleys before the Virginians took up the Buckeye shout, calling on the 84th to "quit firing! You are firing on your own men!"[9]

The 84th, blasting away from the edge of the woods, heard the cry and stopped dead in their tracks. Before Murray and his officers could regain control, the feisty little detachment of the 1st Virginia Battalion fired several crippling volleys. The fire of

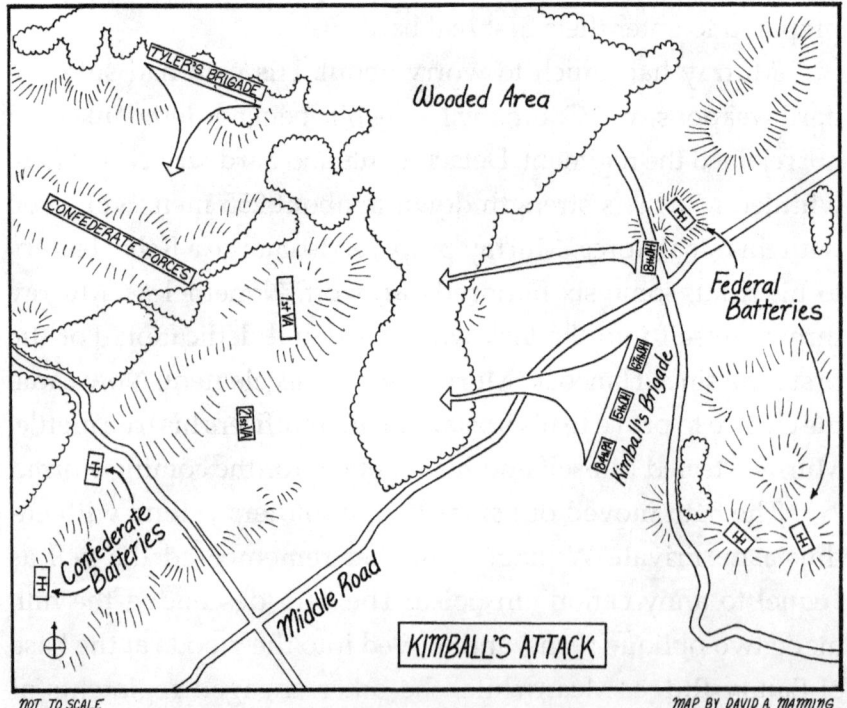

NOT TO SCALE   MAP BY DAVID A. MANNING

four Confederate cannon, situated atop the highest point of Sandy Ridge, also began to play hell in the ranks of the 84th. Several men fell in the storm, including Lieutenant Charles Reem of Company A. Reem, shot through the gut, was the first officer of the 84th to fall that Sunday. He would not be the last.[10]

Murray got his regiment to advance again, but a new threat awaited the Pennsylvanians. Another Confederate regiment, the 21st Virginia, had deployed on their left, behind another stonewall. The 84th Pennsylvania found itself caught in a crossfire: artillery to their front, and infantry fire from both flanks.[11]

Murray and his men found themselves in the very vortex of hell. The 84th's advance again stalled, and the men crouched and returned fire. Murray rode among his men, shouting encouragement. Suddenly, his horse bucked wildly; the animal had been shot. The horse became uncontrollable, and Murray fell from his saddle. The mortally wounded animal ran for the rear, and Murray leaped back onto his feet and surveyed the damage to his beloved regiment.[12]

The 84th melted away in front of Murray's eyes. With no support on either flank, the 84th's situation became dire. Murray exclaimed: "My regiment is all cut to pieces!" and strove to restore order. Indeed, the 84th's casualties grew fearfully every second they stood their ground. Company E, carrying the colors, became a prime target. Color Sergeant Hugh Smith fell with a serious wound, to be followed by four other successive flag bearers. Thomas Gouldsberry, one of only three men of Company I that found their way to the regiment, next picked up the fallen state color and advanced several yards in front of the regiment. Gouldsberry shouted defiance at the Rebels, until his officers ordered him back. Company E's captain, Patrick Gallagher, had been a good friend of Murray's before the war. Earlier in the day, thirty-four-year-old Gallagher had a premonition of his death, and wrote his wife. His premonition came true when a musket ball found his temple and killed him in the front of his company.[13]

Adjutant Thomas Craig and the surviving field officers desperately attempted to get the regiment moving again. Craig, like Murray, rode to the battle mounted. Craig's horse fell as well, and several soldiers of the 84th used the dead animal as a breastwork.[14]

The 84th continued to hold their ground, despite their losses. Murray walked among his soldiers, shouting encouragement and orders, bravely exposing himself to Confederate fire. He determined to prove to his officers his worth as a soldier and as a leader of men in battle. A musket ball struck the top of Murray's kepi, ripping off his oilcloth hat cover. Murray ignored the near miss, brandished his saber, and continued to shout commands and encouragement to his faltering regiment.[15]

Adjutant Craig approached Murray, seeking orders. Murray shouted to his junior officer: "We can hold this place no longer! We must advance or retreat, and we won't retreat!" Craig passed on the order to the surviving company officers, and returned to Murray's side. With a voice "that was heard above the roar of the battle," Murray exclaimed: "Charge, boys charge!"[16]

Across the smoke-shrouded field, a Virginia soldier finished loading his musket and brought the weapon to bear. He aimed his musket at the Yankee lines in front of him, and pulled the trigger. The shot tore across the field, and struck the embossed "84" on the front of Murray's kepi. Continuing on its deadly course, the ball crashed through Murray's skull and passed out the back of his head. Murray toppled backwards, dropping his sword and falling through the folds of the regimental color. Colonel William Gray Murray, businessman, father, and veteran, was dead before he hit the ground.[17]

With Murray's demise, the 84th broke apart and ran for the rear. A few stalwarts, led by 2nd Lieutenant George Zinn, continued to fire from the woods at the crest of the ridge. Had the

The Battle of Kernstown (Winchester), as drawn by Alfred Waud in the April 12, 1862, issue of Harpers Weekly. Note the figure in the center foreground with drawn saber: this is undoubtedly supposed to represent Murray.

© Applewood Books, Inc., Reproduced by permission of Applewood Books and harpersweekly.com

84th held a moment longer they would have seen the 14th Indiana coming to their support. As it stood, the 84th had been too badly mauled to continue. Ninety-two men had been hit, and three officers and twenty enlisted men had been killed outright.[18]

As litter bearers brought Murray's corpse back through the Union lines, a second ball, almost mocking the fallen colonel, struck the dead officer in the thigh. The bearers hurriedly carried Murray's corpse past the onrushing 14th Indiana. As the Hoosiers passed the small party and its grisly burden, they noticed with horror Murray's head wound, which exposed the fallen colonel's brains.[19]

Shields' division, under the leadership of the wily Kimball, emerged victorious that fateful Sunday. The Federals completely drove Jackson's small army from the field, taking more than a hundred prisoners and a few cannon. The 84th led all Federal regiments in killed and wounded. A few days after the battle, in a moment of supreme irony, Captain Horrell pointed out to a New York reporter the spot where Murray fell. Horrell recommended to the reporter that a monument be placed to honor Murray and the 84th in "letters of gold." In death, Murray succeeded in winning over his harshest critic.[20]

CHAPTER 10

Murray's Return

Army undertakers returned Murray's embalmed body to his adopted state of Pennsylvania. His body arrived at Harrisburg on March 26 and lay in state for two full days. Flags flew at half-mast all over the Keystone State. A sad procession carried Murray's body to his mother's residence. Old Sarah Gray Murray, her heart broken, looked one final time on the face of her dead son. One witness to the tragic scene described Murray's countenance as retaining "all its features," and easily "recognizable." The fallen colonel's body spent the night in Harrisburg at Sarah Murray's house.[1]

Murray's flag-draped coffin left Harrisburg at 9:00 a.m. on March 28 aboard a special train dedicated by the Pennsylvania Railroad Company. The train headed for Hollidaysburg, Murray's hometown, stopping in several towns along the way. At each stop, a silent throng waited, heads uncovered, to honor the fallen chieftain. Murray, after all, had been a high-ranking officer, the first Pennsylvania colonel to die in the Rebellion. Pennsylvania, and the country as a whole, had begun to learn the cost of civil war. Newspapers carried accounts of Murray's death in such diverse places as Washington D.C., Chicago, and New York. Few in Pennsylvania suspected just how many other local officers would suffer the same fate in the next three years. The death of a high-ranking Pennsylvania officer would eventually become almost common in the killing fields of Virginia.[2]

Murray's body arrived in Hollidaysburg later that night. A black horse-drawn hearse carried Murray's coffin to the home of John Dougherty, the father of his late wife. Here, Murray's children glimpsed the now lifeless features of their father for the last time. Murray's body remained in state overnight at his father-in-law's house. The next morning, under a gray sky, the friends, associates, and family committed the mortal remains of Colonel William Gray Murray to the earth in a Catholic cemetery in Hollidaysburg. Reverend John Walsh, the man who conducted Murray's wedding, presided over the sad ceremony. With a final salute from the 3rd Pennsylvania, Murray's funeral ended and the crowd dissipated.[3]

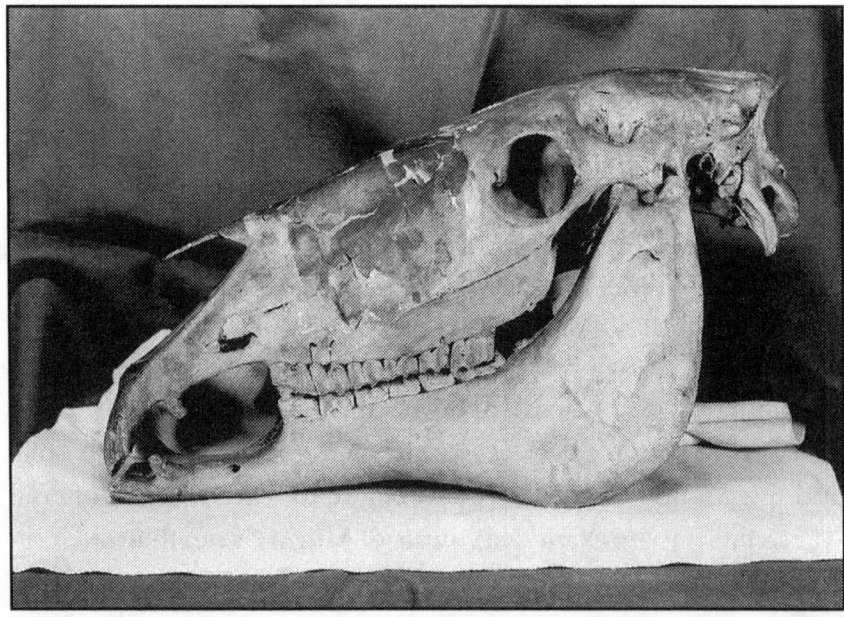

The skull of Murray's horse. Like his master, Murray's charger fell at Kernstown.

Blair County Historical Society

At final rest: the grave of Colonel William Murray, in Hollidaysburg, Pennsylvania.

Author's Collection

Epilogue

Without Murray, the 84th fell apart as a fighting unit. McDowell and Barrett proved to be incapable of leading the regiment, and many of the 84th's captains, the same men who had asked Murray to resign, quit themselves. Governor Curtin appointed Samuel Bowman, a no-nonsense lawyer and self-taught soldier, to clean up the regiment. Bowman eventually turned the 84th into a good outfit, but not without some initial trouble.

Later that summer, in July, Colonel Samuel Sprigg Carrol, the 84th's brigade commander, stood ready to watch the 84th in drill. Before the drill commenced, several company officers reported themselves sick. Carrol, disgusted with the 84th, ordered Bowman to take their names and tie the "sons of bitches up for cowards that wouldn't fight anyway." One young soldier of the 84th, Jacob Wise, stung by Carrol's remarks and the regiment's low reputation, wrote Governor Curtin. Wise asked the governor to both remember the 84th's ordeals and too shield them from hard officers such as Carrol. Wise described the 84th's men as "dull and dissatisfied" with their army service.[1]

In a later part of the letter, Wise remembered another, very different officer. "I don't think Col. Murray will ever be forgotten in the 84th for his kindness to his men during his stay with us. And I don't think the 84th has been the same Reg't ever since he was killed." This tribute becomes William Gray Murray, a brave and gallant officer who sacrificed his life for his regiment and country. It is the sort of tribute that becomes a soldier.[2]

APPENDIX I

Original Organization of the 84th Pennsylvania Volunteers

Field and Staff Officers

Colonel	William Gray Murray
Lieutenant Colonel	Thomas C. McDowell
Major	Walter Barrett
Adjutant	Thomas H. Craig
Quartermaster	John M. Kepheart
Surgeon	Gideon F. Hoop
Assistant Surgeon	C. A. W. Redlick
Chaplain	Alexander McLeod
Sergeant Major	William M. Gwinn
Quartermaster Sergeant	G. A. Ramey
Drum Major	Foster Wighaman
Fife Major	Thaddeus Albert

Line Officers

A Company

Captain	Robert L. Horell
First Lieutenant	Jonathan Derno
Second Lieutenant	Charles Reem

B Company

Captain	Harrison Miles

First Lieutenant   Samuel Bryan
Second Lieutenant   George Zinn

C Company
Captain   Abraham J. Crissman
First Lieutenant   B. M. Morrow
Second Lieutenant   Charles O'Neill

D Company
Captain   Alexander J. Frick
First Lieutenant   Uzal E. Ent
Second Lieutenant   Calvin MacDowell

E Company
Captain   Patrick Gallagher
First Lieutenant   Patrick F. Walsh
Second Lieutenant   John Maloney

F Company
Captain   Robert M. Flack
First Lieutenant   Milton Opp
Second Lieutenant   Jacob Peterman

G Company
Captain   J. Merrick Housler
First Lieutenant   James Ingram
Second Lieutenant   D. N. Taggart

I Company
Captain   Joseph L. Curby
First Lieutenant   Clarence L. Barrett
Second Lieutenant   John W. Paulley

K Company
Captain   Matthew Ogden
First Lieutenant   Charles H. Volk
Second Lieutenant   John W. Taylor

Appendix II

Federal Order of Battle at First Kernstown, March 23 1862

Col. Nathan Kimball, Commanding

FIRST BRIGADE, *Col. Nathan Kimball*
14th Indiana
8th Ohio
67th Ohio
84th Pennsylvania

SECOND BRIGADE, *Col. Jeremiah C. Sullivan*
5th Ohio
13th Indiana
62nd Ohio
39th Illinois

THIRD BRIGADE, *Col. Erastus B. Tyler*
7th Ohio
7th Indiana
1st (Loyal) Virginia
29th Ohio
110th Pennsylvania

CAVALRY, *Col. Thornton F. Brodhead*
1st squadron Ringgold Pennsylvania Cavalry
1st Maryland Cavalry Regiment

1st (Loyal) Virginia Cavalry Battalion
1st Ohio Cavalry (Companies A and D)
1st Michigan Cavalry Battalion

ARTILLERY, *Lt. Col. Philip Daum*
West Virginia Artillery — A Battery
West Virginia Artillery — B Battery
4th US Artillery Regiment — E Battery
1st Ohio Artillery — H Battery
1st Ohio Artillery — L Battery

Notes

Chapter 1

1. Samuel P. Bates, *Martial Deeds of Pennsylvania* (Philadelphia, PA, 1875), p. 541. One other source, the *Altoona Tribune*, April 17, 1862, lists Murray's birth date as July 17, not the 25th.
2. Ibid., p. 541.
3. Ibid.
4. Ibid., p. 542.
5. Ibid.

Chapter 2

1. Murray's Mexican War Service Records, National Archives, Washington, DC, M1028, Roll 11.
2. Murray's Service Records, and Randy W. Hackenburg, *Pennsylvania in the War with Mexico*, (Shippensburg, PA, 1992), p. 257. The enlistment date marks the time when the soldier signed up for the army. The muster in date is when the soldier actually joined his unit and entered the United States Army.
3. Cadmus M. Wilcox, *History of the Mexican War*, (Washington, DC, 1892). Written by the former Confederate general, this fine work has an excellent roster listing all U.S. officers in the Mexican War.
4. Ibid., pp. 7-8.
5. *The Danville Intelligencer*, PA, January, 15, 1847.
6. Hackenburg, p. 14.
7. Ibid., p. 15.
8. Ibid., pp. 15-16.
9. Ibid., p. 16.
10. Ibid., pp. 16-17.
11. Ibid., p. 17.
12. Ibid., pp. 17-18.
13. The dates for Murray's promotion and transfer, both here and below, are taken from his service records in the National Archives.
14. Ibid., pp. 16-20.

Chapter 3

1. There are very few surviving accounts of Murray in the Mexican War. In the Blair County Historical Society, in Altoona, PA, is a GAR Lithograph detailing Murray's Mexican and Civil War service. This lithograph is in error, however, in placing Murray

at the siege of Vera Cruz. Murray did not arrive on the Mexican mainland until after that city had fallen.
2. For reference to these Mexican War actions and the ones below, see Jack K. Bauer, *The Mexican War 1846-1848* (New York, 1974); and John S. D. Eisenhower, *So Far from God; The U.S. War With Mexico* (New York, 1989); Also Edward D. Mansfield, *The Mexican War and a History of its Origins* (Cincinnati, 1849).
3. Murray's Mexican War service lithograph lists Cerro Gordo as a battle in which Murray was present.
4. The order of battle for Cadwalader's brigade is taken from Wilcox, p. 464.
5. Charles Campbell became a brigadier general in the Union army. Two of the 11th's officers became Confederate colonels: John Savage and Arthur C. Cummings. Five other officers, William Irvin, William Gray, John Gregg, Thomas McCoy, and Andrew Tippin, became U.S. colonels. From *Wilcox*, pp. 643-44.
6. Murray's service records, and the regimental papers of the 11th U.S. Volunteers, National Archives.
7. Bauer, pp. 296-301.
8. Ibid., pp. 300-301.
9. Ibid., pp. 306-11. David Nevin, *The Mexican War* (Alexandria, VA), pp. 206-10. Both of these give good accounts of the battle of Molino del Ray.
10. Bauer, p. 310.
11. Nevin, p. 210.
12. Ibid., p. 211.
13. Bauer, pp. 316-18. The other four columns were: four companies of the Voltigeur Regiment under Lt. Col. Joseph Johnston, four other companies of the same regiment under Col. Timothy Andrews, and Shields and Persifor Smith's brigades.
14. Ibid., p. 318.
15. Scott himself courted the Catholic Church while in Mexico. See Eisenhower, pp. 267, 297; Bates, *Martial Deeds*, p. 542.
16. Bates, *Martial Deeds*, p. 542. During June, Scott had sought peace with Mexico. In order to facilitate peace, Santa Anna asked for ten thousand dollars up front, and a million at the signing of the treaty. Scott seriously considered this, and consequently got into trouble with Polk (see Bauer, pp. 284-87). What information the dispatches that Murray carried is unknown.
17. Peace was not formally signed with Mexico until February 2, 1848. Thus, there was still a possible need for more volunteers.
18. Bates, *Martial Deeds*, p. 542.
19. Ibid. Murray's friendship with Scott, who at this time had serious trouble with the Polk administration, may have contributed to the changing of Murray's marching orders.
20. Ibid. The date of Murray's actual resignation is unknown, but was in the summer of 1848.

Chapter 4

1. Ibid. It is not known if Murray had a falling out with Scott. He would later vote against his commander in the election of 1852.
2. Blair County has at least 10 active furnaces at this time, as well as a number of new banks. *Altoona Tribune*, April 9, 1862. William G. Murray's Pension, the National Archives. One other document in Murray's pension lists the marriage date as August 13.
3. Murray Pension, National Archives. U.S. Census Records for Blair County, 1860.

4. Ibid.
5. *Altoona Tribune*, April 17, 1862.
6. Murray Pension File.
7. Bates, *Martial Deeds*, p. 543, and *The Shirleysburg Harold*, PA, April 3, 1862. Information on Sarah Murray taken from the Murray family Bible in the Blair County Historical Society.
8. Murray's Commission in the "Scott Legion" is in the collection of the Blair County Historical Society, in Altoona, PA.
9. William Murray Pension, National Archives. Sarah Gray is listed in the U.S. Census for 1860, so the child must have died soon after that date. It is not known how Sarah died, but the disease that killed Elizabeth Murray is a likely cause.
10. Ibid.
11. Samuel Bates, *History of the Pennsylvania Volunteers*, Philadelphia, PA, 1869, p. 1861, and Bates, *Martial Deeds*, p. 543.
12. *Hollidaysburg Register*, October 2, 1861. Although it cannot be said with complete certainty that Murray authored the article, he is the most likely candidate.

CHAPTER 5

1. *Clearfield Republican*, October 23, 1861.
2. Thomas Merchant, *Eighty-Fourth Pennsylvania Volunteers*, Pennsylvania, 1889 and Harvey Wells, *Philadelphia Weekly Times*, April 10, 1886. The "Mountain Brigade" was proposed by J. Y. James, Ira Mitchell, a "Dr. Forney," and Walter Barrett. Simon Cameron, the secretary of war, authorized its creation.
3. Robert Weidensall, Correspondence, George Williams College, Chicago, Illinois.
4. *Huntingdon Journal and American*, October 15, 1861; Wells, *Philadelphia Weekly Times*, April 10, 1886.
5. *Now and Then*, published by the Muncy County Historical Society. Vol. 12, Issue 12, p. 39. Date unknown, but circa 1965.
6. Weidensall Correspondence. Weidensall was a private in Company A.
7. Bates, *Martial Deeds*, pp. 533–44.
8. Ibid., p. 544.
9. Merchant, p. 17.
10. Wells, *Philadelphia Weekly Times*, April 10, 1886.
11. Ibid.

CHAPTER 6

1. Ibid., and Merchant, pp. 19–29. Also, the *Philadelphia Press*, January 13, 1862.
2. *Muncy Luminary*, January 14, 1862.
3. Merchant, pp. 19–20, and Wells, *Philadelphia Weekly Times*, April 10, 1886; *Columbia County Republican*, January 16, 1862.
4. *Muncy Luminary*, January 1, 1862, and a letter written by Corporal Alexander Read, of Company I, reprinted in the *Clearfield Progress*, April 9, 1961.
5. Charles Clark M.D. (Decker, Frederick Charles, Ed.), *Yates Phalanx: The History of the Thirty-Ninth Regiment, Illinois Volunteer Veteran Infantry, in the War of the Rebellion, 1861–1865*, Chicago, 1889, pp. 23–24.
6. *Philadelphia Press*, January 13, 1862.
7. Report of Colonel T. O. Osborn, 39th Illinois, taken from Clark, pp. 23–25.
8. *Philadelphia Press*, January 13, 1862, *Clearfield Progress*, April 9, 1961, and Osborn's Report, Clark, p. 25.

9. *Muncy Luminary*, January 14, 1862. This letter was written by Harvey Wells.
10. As in so many Civil War affairs, exact times are difficult to ascertain. Corporal Read, quoted in the *Clearfield Progress* (April 9, 1961), wrote that the 84th fell in at five in the morning. Another soldier in the 84th, this one writing in the *Philadelphia Press* (January 13, 1862), claimed the 84th fell in at four o'clock a.m. The later time is, in the opinion of the author, more accurate.
11. *Clearfield Republican*, February 12, 1862.
12. Report of Colonel T. O. Osborn, reprinted in *Yates Phalanx: The History of the 39th Regiment, Illinois Volunteer Veteran Infantry in the War of the Rebellion, 1861–1865*.
13. Clark, p. 21.
14. Alexander Read, quoted in the *Clearfield Progress*, April 9, 1961. Company E's deployment is difficult to determine. No source lists their position, yet they were nonetheless there. From the available evidence, they were in reserve.
15. Weidensall Letters, January 24, 1862; *Clearfield Republican*, February 12, 1862.
16. *Clearfield Republican*, February 12, 1862.
17. *Philadelphia Press*, January 13, 1862.
18. Ibid.
19. Ibid.
20. Report of Orrin Mann, 39th Illinois, contained in Clark, p. 37.
21. *Philadelphia Press*, January 13, 1862, and the *Clearfield Republican*, February 12, 1862.
22. Merchant, p. 23. The death of Theodore Pardee is recorded in a number of period newspaper articles. See the April 9, 1961, issue of the *Clearfield Progress* for Corporal Alexander Read's letter, and the February 12, 1862, soldier's letter in the *Clearfield Republican*.
23. This letter appeared in the April 9, 1961, *Clearfield Progress*.
24. *Clearfield Republican*, February 12, 1862.
25. Evidently, Muhlenburg was successful in driving off the CS guns (Clark, pp. 33–34).
26. *Muncy Luminary*, January 14, 1862.
27. James Hamilton, *Manuscript History of the 110th Pennsylvania*, War Library and Museum, Philadelphia.
28. *Philadelphia Press*, January, 13, 1862.
29. *Clearfield Progress*, April 9, 1961.
30. Clark, p. 34; *Clearfield Republican*, February 12, 1862.
31. *Muncy Luminary*, January 14, 1862.
32. *Columbia County Republican*, January 16, 1862. The Lander quote is taken from a letter that appeared in the *Clearfield Republican*, circa February 20, 1862.

Chapter 7

1. Wells, *Philadelphia Weekly Times*, April 10, 1861.
2. Dave Richards, *Itinerary of the 84th Pennsylvania*.
3. *The Philadelphia Press*, February 25, 1862.
4. Ibid.
5. Ibid.
6. *Clearfield Republican*, circa February 20, 1862, and Richards, *Itinerary*, Also, the *Muncy Luminary*, March 4, 1862.
7. Record Book of the 84th Pennsylvania Volunteers, National Archives. Merchant, p. 27.
8. Richards, *Itinerary*.

Chapter 8

1. Ibid.
2. Copies of both the letter to Murray and Governor Curtin reside in the 84th's Regimental Papers in the Pennsylvania State Archives in Harrisburg.
3. Richards, *Itinerary*.
4. Richards, *Itinerary*. Nathaniel Banks Papers, Library of Congress.
5. Richards, *Itinerary*.
6. A copy of this letter is in the 84th's Regimental Papers, at the Pennsylvania Archives in Harrisburg. The officer's letter to Governor Curtin also contained a list of "offenses." This list, as well as most of the officer's signatures which accompanied it, are conveniently not in the file. In their letter to Governor Curtin, the officers complained that they had never received any battalion drill. The letter has only the signatures of Horrell, Captain Abraham Crissman (Company C), and Captain Alexander Frick (Company D). An attached sheet is missing. Also note that both letters, in Horrell's hand, are very hard to transcribe.
7. Private Letter, Richards Collection.
8. Alpheus Williams, *From the Cannon's Mouth: The Civil War Letters of General Alpheus Williams* (Detroit: Wayne State University Press, 1959), pp. 53–55.

Chapter 9

1. Thomas Craig, "A Delayed Report of the 84th Pa. at Kernstown," *National Tribune*, November 11, 1889, and 84th Pennsylvania Order Book, National Archives.
2. *Clearfield Republican*, April 16, 1862, Richards, *Itinerary*, and William Gallagher's Letters, National Archives.
3. *The War of the Rebellion: A Compilation of the Official Records of the Union and Confederate Armies*, Vol. 12, Series 1, 1880–1901, pp. 338–39.
4. Kimball's Report, *Official Records*, Vol. 12, p. 360, and Gallagher Letter.
5. Gallagher Letter, National Archives. The overall battle accounts are taken from the various accounts in the *Official Records*, pp. 334–411. Additional information can be found in *We Are in For it! The Battle of Kernstown* (Shippensburg, PA: White Mane Publishing Co., Inc., 1998).
6. Kimball's Report, *Official Records*, p. 360.
7. Thomas Fowler, *National Tribune*, May 16, 1889. Murray's exchange with Daum is controversial. Fowler wrote a nonsensical "old soldier" account of Murray arguing with Daum over the use of Chain Shot. In reality, Murray probably asked Daum for artillery support during his advance.
8. McDowell, Thomas letter in the Regimental Papers, in Harrisburg, PA, and Craig, *National Tribune*, November 21, 1889.
9. *Muncy Luminary*, March 31, 1862.
10. Ibid. and the Charles Reem Pension, National Archives.
11. A good account of the 21st Virginia's actions can be found in Colonel John Patton's Report in the *Official Records*, Vol. 12, pp. 402–4.
12. Fowler, *National Tribune*, May 16, 1889, and Craig, *National Tribune*, November 21, 1889. The skull of Murray's horse is in the possession of the Blair County Historical Society.
13. Fowler, *National Tribune*, May 16, 1889, and Craig, *National Tribune*, November 11, 1889. Patrick Gallagher was the writer's great-great-great-grandfather.
14. Craig, *National Tribune*, November 21, 1889.
15. *Altoona Tribune*, March 26, 1862.
16. Ibid., April 3, 1862.

17. Craig, *National Tribune*, November 11, 1889. According to a few other accounts, a spent ball hit Murray in the torso prior to his fatal head wound.
18. Bates, *History of the Pennsylvania Volunteers*, Vol. 2, p. 1862.
19. Augustus M. Van Dyke Letter, March 28, 1862, *Van Dyke Papers*, Folder 1, Indiana Historical Society, Indianapolis, Indiana.
20. *Clearfield Republican*, circa March 26, 1862.

CHAPTER 10

1. *Pennsylvania Telegraph*, Harrisburg, PA, March 26, 1862.
2. Ibid., March 31, 1862.
3. Ibid., Captain Patrick Gallagher, Murray's friend, was laid to rest in Hollidaysburg the same day.

EPILOGUE

1. Jacob Wise Letter, *84th Pennsylvania Regimental Papers*, Harrisburg, PA.
2. Ibid.

BIBLIOGRAPHY

PRIMARY SOURCES

Clark, Charles, M.D. (Decker, Frederick Charles, Ed.) *Yates Phalanx: The History of the Thirty- Ninth Regiment, Illinois Volunteer Veteran Infantry, in the War of the Rebellion, 1861–1865.* Chicago, 1889.

Craig, Thomas. A Delayed Report of the 84th Pa. at Kernstown. *National Tribune*, November 11, 1889; November 21, 1889.

Fowler, Thomas. *National Tribune*, May 16, 1889.

Merchant, Thomas. *Eighty-Fourth Pennsylvania Volunteers.* Pennsylvania, 1889.

Read, Alexander letter. *Clearfield Progress*, April 9, 1961.

Wells, Harvey. *Philadelphia Weekly Times*, April 10, 1886.

Williams, Alpheus. *From the Cannon's Mouth: The Civil War Letters of General Alpheus Williams.* Detroit: Wayne State University Press, 1959.

The War of the Rebellion: A Compilation of the Official Records of the Union and Confederate Armies. Vol. 12, Series 1, 1880–1901.

NEWSPAPERS

Altoona Tribune, March 26, 1862; April 3, 1862; April 9, 1862; April 17, 1862.

Clearfield Progress, April 9, 1961.

Clearfield Republican, October 23, 1861; February 12, 1862; circa February 20, 1862.

Columbia County Republican, January 16, 1862.

The Danville Intelligencer, PA, January 15, 1847.

Hollidaysburg Register, October 2, 1861.

Huntingdon Journal and American, October 15, 1861.

Muncy Luminary, January 1, 1862; January 14, 1862; March 31, 1862.

Pennsylvania Telegraph, March 26, 1862; March 31, 1862.

Philadelphia Press, January 13, 1862; February 25, 1862.

The Shirleysburg Harold, PA, April 3, 1862.

Manuscript Sources

Civil War Library and Museum. Philadelphia, Pennsylvania.

  Hamilton, James. Manuscript History of the 110th Pennsylvania.

Indiana Historical Society. Indianapolis, Indiana.

  Van Dyke, Augustus M. Letter, March 28, 1862. Van Dyke Papers, folder 1.

Library of Congress.

  Nathaniel Banks Papers.

National Archives. Washington, D.C.

  William Gallagher's Civil War Pension File.

  William G. Murray Civil War Pension.

  William G. Murray Mexican War Service Records.

  Charles Reem's Civil War Pension File.

  U.S. Census Records for Blair County, 1860.

  Record Book of the 84th Pennsylvania Volunteers.

Pennsylvania State Records. Harrisburg, Pennsylvania.

  84th Pennsylvania Volunteer Regimental Papers. Harrisburg, PA.

Williams College. Chicago, Illinois.

Weidensall, Robert Correspondence.

SECONDARY SOURCES

Bates, Samuel. *History of the Pennsylvania Volunteers*. Philadelphia, PA: B. Singerly, 1869.

Bates, Samuel P. *Martial Deeds of Pennsylvania*. Philadelphia, PA: T. H. Davis & Co., 1875.

Bauer, K. Jack. *The Mexican War 1846-1848*. New York: Macmillan Publishing Co., Inc., 1974.

Ecelbarger, Gary. *We Are in For it! The Battle of Kernstown*. Shippensburg, PA: White Mane Publishing Co., Inc., 1998.

Eisenhower, John S. D. *So Far from God; The U.S. War with Mexico*. New York: Anchor Books, 1989.

Hackenburg, Randy W. *Pennsylvania in the War with Mexico*. Shippensburg, PA: White Mane Publishing Co., Inc., 1992.

Mansfield, Edward D. *The Mexican War and a History of its Origins*. Cincinnati: A. S. Barnes & Co., 1849.

Muncy County Historical Society, *Now and Then*. Vol. 12, Issue 12, c. 1965.

Nevin, David. *The Mexican War*. Alexandria, VA: Time Life Books, c. 1975.

Wilcox, Cadmus M. *History of the Mexican War*. Washington, D.C.: Church News Publishing Co., 1892.

INDEX

A
Alpine Station, Maryland, 39–41
Ashby, Turner, 36–42, 50

B
Baltimore and Ohio Railroad, 34, 43
Banks, Nathaniel, 49, 55
Barrett, Walter, 31–32, 40, 45, 51, 67
Blake, Samuel, 35–36
Bowman, Samuel, 67
Bryan, Samuel, 28
Buchanan, James, 23–24
Buena Vista, Battle of, 4
Bunker Hill, Virginia, 49

C
Cadwalader, George, 11
Cameron, Simon, 4, 75n
Cameron Guards, 4
Camp Crossman, Pennsylvania. 27–28, 30, 33
Camp Curtin, Pennsylvania, 30, 41, 45
Camp Kelley, Virginia, 46
Camp Kimball, Virginia, 49–50
Canandaigua, New York, 1
Carrol, Samuel Sprigg, 67
Cerro Gordo, Battle of, 11
Chapultepec, Battle of, 16–18
Chesapeake and Ohio Canal, 34
Churubusco, Battle of, 14–15
Clear Spring, Maryland, 33
Contreras, Battle of, 13
Craig, Thomas H., 32, 60
Crissman, Abraham, 77n
Cumberland, Maryland, 37, 39, 45–46
Curtin, Andrew, 24, 30, 67

D
Daugherty, John, 21, 64
Daum, Philip, 57, 77n
Derno, Jonathan, 37–38

E
8th Ohio Volunteer Infantry, 55–57
84th Pennsylvania Volunteer Infantry
  formed and organized, 27–32
  at Hancock action, 34–43
  inexperience of, 31, 33
  issued Belgian muskets, 34–35
  Kernstown Battle, 53–62
  officers' revolt of, 51–52
  pay issues, 46

F
5th Ohio Infantry Regiment, 58
First Bull Run, Battle of, 24
1st Virginia Battalion (C.S.), 58
Fort Hamilton, New York, 19
Fort McHenry, Maryland, 19
14th Indiana Volunteer Infantry, 46, 57–58
Frick, Alexander, 77n

G
Gallagher, Patrick, 40, 59–60, 77n
Gallagher, William, 56–57
Gouldsberry, Thomas, 59

H
Hagerstown, Maryland, 32, 41
Hancock, Maryland, 34–43
Harrisburg, Pennsylvania, 2, 4, 30, 31, 32, 57, 63
Hill, Daniel Harvey, 16, 17
Hollidaysburg, Pennsylvania, 22, 23, 25–26, 63–64
Hoop, Gideon, 38
Horrell, Robert, 50, 62, 77n
Houck, Darsey, 31
Huntingdon, Pennsylvania, 27

J
Jackson, Thomas Jonathan, 17, 34, 37, 41–43, 49, 56, 62

Index

James, J. Y., 27

K

Kernstown, Battle of, 53–61
Kimball, Nathan, 46, 47, 49–50, 53, 55–58, 62

L

Lander, Frederick West, 41–43, 47–48
Landis, J. A., 24
Lee, Robert E., 13
Lewis, William, 27, 45
Lobos, Mexico, 6–7
Longford, Ireland, 1

M

MacDowell, Thomas C., 31, 67
Maloney, John, 50
Mann, Orrin, 36–37, 42
Marcy, William, 18
Martinsburg, Virginia, 49
Mexico City, Mexico, 11–18
Molino del Ray, Battle of, 16
Muhlenburg, E. D., 36–40
Murray, Elizabeth (Daugherty) (wife), 21, 23
   death of, 24
Murray, John (father), 1–2
Murray, John Bartholomew (son), 23
Murray, Mary Carmel (daughter), 23
Murray, William Gray
   asked to resign, 50–52
   at Battle of Kernstown, 53–62
   commissioned colonel, 24–25
   death of, 60
   early life, 1–2
   enlists in Regular Army, 9, 11
   funeral of, 63–64
   at Hancock, 33–43
   inflammatory rheumatism of, 46
   Mexican War service, 3–19
   postmaster of Hollidaysburg, Pennsylvania, 23–24
   writes newspaper letter, 25–26
Murray, Sarah (mother), 1, 63
Murray, Sarah Gray (daughter), 23
   death of, 24

N

New Orleans, Louisiana, 5–6
New York, New York, 1–2, 63

O

O'Friel, Catharine, 23
Oldtown, Maryland, 47
110th Pennsylvania Volunteer Infantry
   formed and organized, 27–28
   inexperience of, 33, 41
   plans to attack the 84th Pennsylvania, 28
   rioting of, 41
Osborn, Thomas, 36

P

Panic of 1837, 1–2
Pardee, Theodore, 39–40
Perote, Mexico, 13
Philadelphia, Pennsylvania, 18, 24, 28, 41
Pierce, Franklin, 23
Pillow, Gideon, 12
Polk, James, 4, 18

Q

Quitman, John, 17

R

Reem, Charles, 59
Rome, New York, 1

S

San Agustin, Mexico, 13
Santa Anna, Antonio Lopez de, 4, 14–15
Scott Legion, 24
Scott, Winfield, 11–19
   relationship with Murray, 18
2nd Pennsylvania Volunteer Infantry (Mexican War), 3–11
7th Loyal Virginia Infantry (U.S), 46
7th Virginia Cavalry (C.S.), 39, 55
Sir John's Run, skirmish at, 36–38
67th Ohio Volunteer Infantry, 57
Shields, James, 43, 53
   wounded at Kernstown, 55
Smith, Hugh, 59
Stokes, Ned, 31
Strasburg, Virginia, 50
Sullivan, Jeremiah, 55–56

T

Tacubaya Armistice, 15
Taylor, Zachary, 3–4, 11
Texas, 3–4
13th Indiana Volunteer Infantry, 14
39th Illinois Volunteer Infantry, 35–40
Trist Mission, 15
Trousdale, William B., 17
21st Virginia Infantry (C.S.), 59
Tyler, Erastus, 56

U

U.S. Army
   11th U.S. Infantry Regiment (Mexican War), 9–19, 74n

Index

4th U.S. Artillery Regiment (Mexican War), 16
4th U.S. Artillery Regiment, Battery K, 36–38
14th U.S. Infantry Regiment (Mexican War), 17
U.S. Navy
   USS *Anthony Wayne*, 5
   USS *General Veazie*, 6–8
Utica, New York, 1

V

Vera Cruz, Mexico, 8–9, 11–13, 73n
Voltigeur Regiment, 12, 74n

W

Walsh, John, 21, 64
Warm Springs Ridge, action at, 37–38
Wells, Harvey, 28, 33, 46
Williams, Alpheus, 52
Williams, Edward C., 4
Williamsport, Maryland, 41
Winchester, Virginia, 49–50, 53, 55
Wise, Jacob, 67
Worth, William, 16

Z

Ziegler, Jacob, 27
Zinn, George, 60

— OF RELATED INTEREST —

WE MIGHT AS WELL DIE HERE
The 53d Pennsylvania Veteran Volunteer Infantry
Irvin G. Myers

The 53d Pennsylvania was a fighting regiment in a fighting division of a fighting corps—and their colonel, John R. Brooke, one of the best of the young leaders who came to the fore under the stern but inspirational tutelage of "Hancock the Superb."

ISBN-10 1-57249-375-5 • ISBN-13 978-1-57249-375-9
Softcover $27.95

THE FORGOTTEN CHARGE
*The 123rd Pennsylvania at
Marye's Heights, Fredericksburg, Virginia*
Scott B. Lang

The Forgotten Charge relates the common soldiers' perspective of the Army of the Potomac's failures from August 1862 to May 1863. Scott Lang recounts the regiment's baptism of fire during the charge on Marye's Heights and the disappointments that followed during the subsequent months.

ISBN-10 1-57249-292-9 • ISBN-13 978-1-57249-292-9
Softcover $12.95

BOUQUETS FROM THE CANNON'S MOUTH
*Soldiering with the Eighth Regiment
of the Pennsylvania Reserves*
Robert E. Eberly, Jr.

Focusing primarily on five young volunteers, the author tells the story of the Eighth Regiment of the Pennsylvania Reserves from the Seven Days Battles to the siege of Petersburg where four of the five were captured and sent to the Confederate prison at Salisbury, North Carolina. Incorporating two rare prison diaries, ten maps, six appendices, and numerous photographs, this book, as Edwin C. Bearss notes in his foreword, is for those "who savor the soldiers' story."

ISBN-10 1-57249-373-9 • ISBN-13 978-1-57249-373-5
Hardcover $34.95

FOR HONOR, FLAG, AND FAMILY
Civil War Major General Samuel W. Crawford, 1827–1892
Richard Wagner

For Honor, Flag, and Family shows the depth of compassion and the complexity of character that led to the prominence of Samuel Crawford, the highest-ranking officer from Franklin County, Pennsylvania. While serving at Fort Sumter, he eloquently delivered his lifelong motto: "I must sustain with honor my flag and the reputation of the name I bear."

ISBN-10 1-57249-372-0 • ISBN-13 978-1-57249-372-8
Softcover $19.95

— The Author —

Roderick Gainer is a contract historian and collections analyst for the U.S. Army Center of Military History. He obtained a bachelor's degree in history from Arizona State University and studied under Joseph Harsh while obtaining his master's degree from George Mason University in Virginia. Mr. Gainer regularly conducts tours and battlefield staff rides in both Europe and the United States.

— Cover Illustration —
Colonel William Gray Murray
Blair County Historical Society

White Mane Publishing Co., Inc.

To Request a Catalog Please Write to:
WHITE MANE PUBLISHING COMPANY, INC.
P.O. Box 708 • Shippensburg, PA 17257
e-mail: marketing@whitemane.com
Cover Design by Angela Guyer

www.ingramcontent.com/pod-product-compliance
Lightning Source LLC
Chambersburg PA
CBHW031653040426
42453CB00006B/299